LAYERS OF LEARNING

YEAR FOUR • UNIT TWO

EXPANDING NATION

PACIFIC STATES

MOTORS & ENGINES

TALL TALES

Published by HooDoo Publishing
United States of America
© 2016 Layers of Learning
ISBN 978-1534725782

Units at a Glance: Topics For All Four Years of the Layers of Learning Program

1	History	Geography	Science	The Arts
1	Mesopotamia	Maps & Globes	Planets	Cave Paintings
2	Egypt	Map Keys	Stars	Egyptian Art
3	Europe	Global Grids	Earth & Moon	Crafts
4	Ancient Greece	Wonders	Satellites	Greek Art
5	Babylon	Mapping People	Humans in Space	Poetry
6	The Levant	Physical Earth	Laws of Motion	List Poems
7	Phoenicians	Oceans	Motion	Moral Stories
8	Assyrians	Deserts	Fluids	Rhythm
9	Persians	Arctic	Waves	Melody
10	Ancient China	Forests	Machines	Chinese Art
11	Early Japan	Mountains	States of Matter	Line & Shape
12	Arabia	Rivers & Lakes	Atoms	Color & Value
13	Ancient India	Grasslands	Elements	Texture & Form
14	Ancient Africa	Africa	Bonding	African Tales
15	First North Americans	North America	Salts	Creative Kids
16	Ancient South America	South America	Plants	South American Art
17	Celts	Europe	Flowering Plants	Jewelry
18	Roman Republic	Asia	Trees	Roman Art
19	Christianity	Australia & Oceania	Simple Plants	Instruments
20	Roman Empire	You Explore	Fungi	Composing Music

2	History	Geography	Science	The Arts
1	Byzantines	Turkey	Climate & Seasons	Byzantine Art
2	Barbarians	Ireland	Forecasting	Illumination
3	Islam	Arabian Peninsula	Clouds & Precipitation	Creative Kids
4	Vikings	Norway	Special Effects	Viking Art
5	Anglo Saxons	Britain	Wild Weather	King Arthur Tales
6	Charlemagne	France	Cells & DNA	Carolingian Art
7	Normans	Nigeria	Skeletons	Canterbury Tales
8	Feudal System	Germany	Muscles, Skin, Cardio	Gothic Art
9	Crusades	Balkans	Digestive & Senses	Religious Art
10	Burgundy, Venice, Spain	Switzerland	Nerves	Oil Paints
11	Wars of the Roses	Russia	Health	Minstrels & Plays
12	Eastern Europe	Hungary	Metals	Printmaking
13	African Kingdoms	Mali	Carbon Chemistry	Textiles
14	Asian Kingdoms	Southeast Asia	Non-metals	Vivid Language
15	Mongols	Caucasus	Gases	Fun With Poetry
16	Medieval China & Japan	China	Electricity	Asian Arts
17	Pacific Peoples	Micronesia	Circuits	Arts of the Islands
18	American Peoples	Canada	Technology	Indian Legends
19	The Renaissance	Italy	Magnetism	Renaissance Art I
20	Explorers	Caribbean Sea	Motors	Renaissance Art II

www.Layers-of-Learning.com

3	History	Geography	Science	The Arts
1	Age of Exploration	Argentina & Chile	Classification & Insects	Fairy Tales
2	The Ottoman Empire	Egypt & Libya	Reptiles & Amphibians	Poetry
3	Mogul Empire	Pakistan & Afghanistan	Fish	Mogul Arts
4	Reformation	Angola & Zambia	Birds	Reformation Art
5	Renaissance England	Tanzania & Kenya	Mammals & Primates	Shakespeare
6	Thirty Years' War	Spain	Sound	Baroque Music
7	The Dutch	Netherlands	Light & Optics	Baroque Art I
8	France	Indonesia	Bending Light	Baroque Art II
9	The Enlightenment	Korean Peninsula	Color	Art Journaling
10	Russia & Prussia	Central Asia	History of Science	Watercolors
11	Conquistadors	Baltic States	Igneous Rocks	Creative Kids
12	Settlers	Peru & Bolivia	Sedimentary Rocks	Native American Art
13	13 Colonies	Central America	Metamorphic Rocks	Settler Sayings
14	Slave Trade	Brazil	Gems & Minerals	Colonial Art
15	The South Pacific	Australasia	Fossils	Principles of Art
16	The British in India	India	Chemical Reactions	Classical Music
17	The Boston Tea Party	Japan	Reversible Reactions	Folk Music
18	Founding Fathers	Iran	Compounds & Solutions	Rococo
19	Declaring Independence	Samoa & Tonga	Oxidation & Reduction	Creative Crafts I
20	The American Revolution	South Africa	Acids & Bases	Creative Crafts II

4	History	Geography	Science	The Arts
1	American Government	USA	Heat & Temperature	Patriotic Music
2	Expanding Nation	Pacific States	Motors & Engines	Tall Tales
3	Industrial Revolution	U.S. Landscapes	Energy	Romantic Art I
4	Revolutions	Mountain West States	Energy Sources	Romantic Art II
5	Africa	U.S. Political Maps	Energy Conversion	Impressionism I
6	The West	Southwest States	Earth Structure	Impressionism II
7	Civil War	National Parks	Plate Tectonics	Post Impressionism
8	World War I	Plains States	Earthquakes	Expressionism
9	Totalitarianism	U.S. Economics	Volcanoes	Abstract Art
10	Great Depression	Heartland States	Mountain Building	Kinds of Art
11	World War II	Symbols & Landmarks	Chemistry of Air & Water	War Art
12	Modern East Asia	The South	Food Chemistry	Modern Art
13	India's Independence	People of America	Industry	Pop Art
14	Israel	Appalachian States	Chemistry of Farming	Modern Music
15	Cold War	U.S. Territories	Chemistry of Medicine	Free Verse
16	Vietnam War	Atlantic States	Food Chains	Photography
17	Latin America	New England States	Animal Groups	Latin American Art
18	Civil Rights	Home State Study I	Instincts	Theater & Film
19	Technology	Home State Study II	Habitats	Architecture
20	Terrorism	America in Review	Conservation	Creative Kids

Unit 4-2 Printable Pack

This unit includes printables at the end. To make life easier for you we also created digital printable packs for each unit. To retrieve your printable pack for Unit 4-2, please visit

www.layers-of-learning.com/digital-printable-packs/

Put the printable pack in your shopping cart and use this coupon code:

615UNIT4-2

Your printable pack will be free.

Layers of Learning Introduction

This is part of a series of units in the Layers of Learning homeschool curriculum, including the subjects of history, geography, science, and the arts. Children from 1st through 12th can participate in the same curriculum at the same time - family school style.

The units are intended to be used in order as the basis of a complete curriculum (once you add in a systematic math, reading, and writing program). You begin with Year 1 Unit 1 no matter what ages your children are. Spend about 2 weeks on each unit. You pick and choose the activities within the unit that appeal to you and read the books from the book list that are available to you or find others on the same topic from your library. We highly recommend that you use the timeline in every history section as the backbone. Then flesh out your learning with reading and activities that highlight the topics you think are the most important.

Alternatively, you can use the units as activity ideas to supplement another curriculum in any order you wish. You can still use them with all ages of children at the same time.

When you've finished with Year One, move on to Year Two, Year Three, and Year Four. Then begin again with Year One and work your way through the years again. Now your children will be older, reading more involved books, and writing more in depth. When you have completed the sequence for the second time, you start again on it for the third and final time. If your student began with Layers of Learning in 1st grade and stayed with it all the way through she would go through the four year rotation three times, firmly cementing the information in her mind in ever increasing depth. At each level you should expect increasing amounts of outside reading and writing. High schoolers in particular should be reading extensively, and if possible, participating in discussion groups.

These icons will guide you in spotting activities and books that are appropriate for the age of child you are working with. But if you think an activity is too juvenile or too difficult for your kids, adjust accordingly. The icons are not there as rules, just guides.

☺ 1st-4th

☻ 5th-8th

☻ 9th-12th

Within each unit we share:

EXPLORATIONS, activities relating to the topic;
EXPERIMENTS, usually associated with science topics;
EXPEDITIONS, field trips;
EXPLANATIONS, teacher helps or educational philosophies.

In the sidebars we also include Additional Layers, Famous Folks, Fabulous Facts, On the Web, and other extra related topics that can take you off on tangents, exploring the world and your interests with a bit more freedom. The curriculum will always be there to pull you back on track when you're ready.

www.layers-of-learning.com/layers-of-learning-program

UNIT TWO
EXPANDING NATION - PACIFIC - MOTORS & ENGINES - TALL TALES

There are those, I know, who will say that the liberation of humanity, the freedom of man and mind, is nothing but a dream. They are right. It is the American dream.
-Archibald MacLeish, poet, playwright, Librarian of Congress

LIBRARY LIST

HISTORY

Search for: Daniel Boone, Louisiana Purchase, Lewis & Clark, War of 1812, Republic of Texas, Alamo, Trail of Tears, Monroe Doctrine, Indian Wars

☺ A Picture Book of Daniel Boone by David A. Adler.

☺ Lewis and Clark: A Prairie Dog For the President by Shirley Ray Redmond.

☺ The Star Spangled Banner by Peter Spier.

☺ The Town That Fooled the British: A War of 1812 Story by Lisa Papp.

☺ Trail of Tears by Joseph Bruchac.

☺ ☻ Susanna of the Alamo by John Jakes.

☺ ☻ The Story of Texas by John Edward Weems.

☺ ☻ The Boy in the Alamo by Margaret Cousins. Historical fiction.

☺ ☻ If You Lived With the Cherokee by Peter Roop.

☺ ☻ Daniel Boone: Young Hunter and Tracker by Augusta Stevenson. This is part of the excellent "Childhood of Famous Americans" series. Look for other titles in this series all through this year.

☺ ☻ Louisiana Purchase by Peter and Connie Roop.

☺ ☻ How We Crossed the West: The Adventures of Lewis and Clark by Rosalyn Schanzer.

☺ ☻ The Lewis and Clark Expedition by Jessica Gunderson. A graphic history.

☺ ☻ Soft Rain: A Story of the Trail of Tears by Cornelia Cornelissen. Historical novel.

☺ ☻ Make Way For Sam Houston by Jean Fritz.

☻ The Captain's Dog by Roland Smith.

☺ ☻ Sacajawea by Joseph Bruchac. A well-told historical novel.

☻ A Wilderness So Immense: The Louisiana Purchase and the Destiny of America by Jon Kukla. Excellently and grippingly written.

☻ Undaunted Courage: Meriwether Lewis, Thomas Jefferson, and the Opening of the American West by Stephen Ambrose.

☻ Sacajawea by Anna L. Waldo. At more than 1,400 pages, this historical novel is for good readers, but it is a well told and life changing story.

☻ 1812: The War That Forged a Nation by Walter R. Borneman.

GEOGRAPHY	Search for: U.S. States, 50 states, California, Washington, Oregon, Hawaii, Alaska ☺ ☺ ☻ <u>Our California</u> by Pam Munoz Ryan. ☻ <u>"G" Is For Golden: A California Alphabet</u> by David Domeniconi and Pam Carroll. ☻ <u>"E" Is For Evergreen: A Washington State Alphabet</u> by Roland Smith and Linda Holt Ayriss. ☻ <u>"B" Is For Beaver: An Oregon Alphabet</u> by Marie Smith, Roland Smith, and Michael Roydon. ☺ ☻ <u>This is San Francisco</u> by Miroslav Sasek. ☺ ☻ <u>Oregon</u> by Tanya Lloyd Kyi. ☺ ☻ <u>State Shapes: California</u> by Erik Brunn and Rick Peterson. ☺ ☻ <u>State Shapes: Washington</u> by Erin McHugh. ☺ ☻ <u>California History For Kids</u> by Katy S. Duffield. Information plus activities.
SCIENCE	Search for: electric motors, engines, steam engines, internal combustion engine, jets ☺ ☺ ☻ <u>The New Way Things Work</u> by David Macaulay. Packed with lots of physics topics, including motors and engines, this book will fascinate your child. ☻ <u>Steam, Smoke, and Steel</u> by Patrick O'Brien. This book is mostly about the history of trains told in an engaging way for younger kids. ☺ ☻ <u>How Cars Work: The Interactive Guide to Mechanisms That Make A Car Move</u> by Nick Arnold. Comes with pieces that kids put together to make moving models that really show how car parts work from pistons to brakes. ☺ ☻ <u>Car Science</u> by Richard Hammond. From DK, this book is visually amazing and packed with facts from how a car works to how gasoline is made. ☺ ☻ <u>The Boys' Book of Motors, Engines, and Turbines</u> by Alfred Morgan. First published in the 1940's, this book is long out of print, but it's a gem. Find one if you can. ☺ ☻ <u>How Stuff Works</u> by Marshall Brain. Contains lots of topics, one of which is motors and engines. ☻ <u>How Cars Work</u> by Tom Newton. This book is very thorough, but also simple.
THE ARTS	Search for: tall tales, Mike Fink, Pecos Bill, Paul Bunyan, Davy Crockett, Johnny Appleseed, John Henry, Daniel Boone, Calamity Jane, Casey Jones, Stormalong, Flatboat Annie ☺ ☺ ☻ <u>American Tall Tales</u> by Mary Pope Osborne. ☺ ☺ ☻ <u>American Tall Tales</u> by Adrien Stoutenburg. ☺ ☺ ☻ <u>Cut From The Same Cloth: American Women of Myth, Legend, and Tall Tale</u> by Robert D. San Souci. ☺ ☻ <u>Paul Bunyan</u> by Steven Kellogg. Look for others by this author. ☺ ☻ <u>John Henry</u> by Julius Lester. ☺ ☻ <u>John Henry</u> by Ezra Jack Keats. ☺ ☻ <u>Johnny Appleseed</u> by Reeve Lindbergh. ☺ ☻ <u>Paul Bunyan</u> by Steven Krensky. ☺ ☻ <u>The Story of Paul Bunyan</u> by Barbara Emberly. ☺ ☻ <u>Pecos Bill: the Greatest Cowboy of All Time</u> by James Cloyd Bowman.

HISTORY: EXPANDING NATION

Teaching Tip

This is a unit where the timeline is essential. Without a timeline, it will be hard to connect the Lewis and Clark expedition to the War of 1812 to the Battle of the Alamo to the Trail of Tears, and yet these events are connected because they stem from and determine the geography and politics of the United States.

Use the timeline not just as a visual representation of events, but as a teaching tool to help your kids make mental connections between events that are often taught in isolation.

For example, how is the War of 1812 related to the settlement of Daniel Boone and how are Boone and the Louisiana Purchase related to the Trail of Tears?

These four events are connected because the War of 1812 and the Louisiana Purchase created lands for settlers to move westward into and also created an "Indian Territory" for the Trail of Tears destination.

You need a timeline to see these connections.

After the Constitutional Convention settled down, America was just getting started. Immediately factions sprung up and Europe was intruding again. By the end of Washington's presidency two main political parties had emerged, the Federalists and the Democratic-Republicans. In 1798 the United States was having its first constitutional crisis as the Adams administration passed the Alien and Sedition Acts during the scare of the Quasi-War with France. The Alien and Sedition Acts were supposed to protect the government from armed rebellion on the part of newly immigrated French, and indeed, many states were threatening to secede over the political differences between the Federalists, who sided with the British, and Anti-Federalists, who sided with the French. But the Acts gave the president the power to detain and deport resident aliens who were suspected to be dangers to the state or whose country was at war with the United States. Furthermore, it made writing "false, scandalous, and malicious" articles against the federal government or officials to be illegal and punishable. The Acts prompted Jefferson to write a response in the form of the Virginia and Kentucky Resolutions which argued that states were free to refuse to uphold any law that was unconstitutional within their boundaries. Jefferson won the next election, which was hotly contested, primarily over this issue.

The Americans had chosen neutrality in the conflict of the French Revolution, and again decided to remain officially neutral during the Napoleonic Wars, but making France a favored trade partner definitely helped out Napoleon's bottom line. The United States didn't have to officially declare sides to financially support the French, instead completing the Louisiana Purchase. The upshot is that the new nation, whatever it did, acted in its own interest and did not get involved in picking sides in European posturing for power. This attitude came to a pointed head in 1823 with the issuing of the Monroe Doctrine, which warned Europeans to stay out of the western hemisphere and promised that America would stay out of Europe. Of course, America was relatively weak at that time and had no way to enforce any such thing. Fortunately, Britain agreed and used her ships to enforce both the Freedom of the Americas and laissez faire trade around the world, which was just then coming into fashion.

America's goal of neutrality and the avoidance of European conflicts failed in 1812 after the British continued to obstruct American trade with France, illegally impress American sailors, and aid the Native American tribes in warring against American westward settlement. The Americans hoped that the war would also be the opening Canada was waiting for to break free of the British. Canada wanted no such thing and fought for her king and against the American invasion. The Canadians today still consider they won that war since America did not, in fact, win any Canadian territory. America eventually won the war in 1814, kicking the British out for the last time, securing her rights at sea, and settling the question of future European bullying.

This is a painting of Daniel Boone escorting settlers through the Cumberland Gap to settle in what is now Kentucky. Painting by George Caleb Bingham.

In the early 1800's America expanded west very quickly as settlers left the increasingly crowded eastern seaboard for land and space across the Appalachians. The Louisiana Purchase in 1803 more than doubled the U.S. territory. Further territory was added as Texas and California, and finally the United States itself, declared independence from and fought battles against Mexico's chaotic and oppressive government. American settlers poured into these new lands by the thousands.

But the land wasn't empty; it was already inhabited by native tribes. Some of the tribal land was purchased or acquired by treaty with the tribes, but much of it was simply taken in battle or through forced relocations. The Native Americans fought back in many cases, notably the Seminoles in Florida and the Northwest Tribes of the Ohio Valley. Wars on the plains would last until the late 1800's.

Memorization Station

Memorize the presidents of the United States in order.

Here are some printable cards with the names and portraits of each president to help you memorize.

http://www.lay-ers-of-learning.com/memorize-the-presidents-printable-cards/

Famous Folks

Daniel Boone is considered a folk hero, one of the earliest in American history. His exploits were famous during his lifetime and some of the tales about him grew to legend status.

Fabulous Fact

Laissez faire means "let go." It meant free trade between nations, unhindered by government regulations, tariffs, and subsidies.

Fabulous Fact

There was an earlier Northwest Ordinance of 1784, written and championed by Thomas Jefferson, that divided the new land west of the Appalachians into states, giving them equal status with the original states, and declaring them forever slave free. Except the last clause, ending the spread of slavery, was defeated by one vote in the congress. Jefferson bitterly lamented this all his life. Not able to end slavery through legislative means, Jefferson said, "We must hope that an overruling Providence is preparing the deliverance of these our suffering brethren."

On the Web

Here is a 10 minute retro clip introducing the Kentucky pioneers and their daily life.

https://www.youtube.com/watch?v=eV-VjCRWkNZI

And this one is about Daniel Boone's later life, after he moved west to Missouri.

https://www.youtube.com/watch?v=0KQv14Om-78

☺ ☺ ☻ EXPLORATION: Timeline

- 1787 Northwest Ordinance allows white settlement in areas formerly owned by Native American tribes who had sided with the British during the Revolution
- 1787-1795 Northwest Indian War
- 1795 Treaty of Greenville deprives twelve northwest Native American nations of their lands
- 1803 Louisiana Purchase
- 1804 End of slavery north of the Mason-Dixon line
- 1805 Lewis & Clark Expedition reaches the Pacific
- 1808 Slave trade becomes illegal in American and British law
- 1812-1814 War of 1812
- Aug 1814 British burn Washington D.C., including the White House
- 1818 War against the Seminoles in Florida
- 1818 Treaty between U.S. and Britain makes the 49th parallel the border between U.S. and Canada in the west
- 1819 Spain gives Florida to the U.S.
- 1820 Settlers reach the Mississippi
- 1821 There are now 23 states
- 1823 Monroe Doctrine issued
- 1829 Andrew Jackson is president
- 1830 Indian Removal Act legalizes eviction of Native American tribes
- 1835 Texas declares its independence from Mexico
- February 23-March 6, 1835 Battle of the Alamo, Texans defeated, but their brave resistance makes them a rallying call
- 1838-39 "Trail of Tears" moves Cherokee to Oklahoma
- 1842 Treaty between Britain and the United States defines the Maine border
- 1845 Texas votes to become the 28th U.S. state
- 1846 49th parallel border extended across Oregon Country all the way to the Pacific
- 1847 U.S. Army captures Mexico City during the Mexican-American War, giving America huge territories in Utah, California, New Mexico, Arizona, Colorado, and Texas.
- 1853 Gadsden Purchase
- 1867 U.S. buys Alaska from Russia

☺ ☻ EXPLORATION: Daniel Boone

Daniel Boone was one of the earliest explorers, adventurers, hunters, and settlers to move west of the Appalachian Mountains. He and other men like him were instrumental in paving the way for hundreds of thousands of pioneer families to settle in Kentucky, Tennessee, and the Ohio River Valley. Check out some books from the library or internet about Daniel Boone. We like the story of the capture and rescue of Jemima Boone. Have a costume ready to go so your kids can head to the "wilderness"

and replay the blazing of the Wilderness Road.

Daniel Boone wore a fringed shirt, fringed pants, and a beaver hat. Of course, he always carried a rifle too. Buy a tan or brown collared shirt in a size too large for your child. Cut a 3 inch strip off the bottom of the shirt all the way around. Snip the cut side of the strip into fringes, Sew or use no-sew fusible tape to attach the fringe all the way around the shirt across the chest and shoulders. Leave the shirt untucked, but belted at the waist. Add a hat (cowboy, boonie, or beaver) and a toy rifle to the costume. Daniel Boone is often shown wearing a coon skin cap, though he didn't actually wear one in real life.

As you "trailblaze," become a tracker. In the country, this may involve looking for animal tracks and scat, searching for edible plants, and listening for animals. In the city you can search for dog tracks, scat, and bird feathers. Search for evidence of squirrels. Find acorns, dandelion greens, or clover. Compare people tracks from footprints to bike tracks to car tire tracks. You can also check out books from the library about animal tracks to examine while you're on your journey.

☺ ☺ EXPLORATION: Lewis & Clark
Print the Lewis and Clark Expedition Map from the end of this unit, and trace their route as they explored the west. You'll see numbers at each featured location on the map. When you get to each number read the information below.

1. The company assembled at St. Charles, Missouri and included more than 45 men, mostly soldiers, but also French boatmen, and York, Clark's black slave. Lewis also brought his black Newfoundland Dog, Seaman, who would make the entire trip to the Pacific and back. The plan was to make as much of the expedition by boat as possible. At the beginning of the journey they used keel boats, which had a shallow keel

Fabulous Fact
The Indians called the rich, fertile Kentucky Territory a "dark ground" because it was constantly a battlefield where tribes competed for control of the land. At the time of Daniel Boone, no tribe owned the land.

Additional Layer
In his childhood Daniel Boone made friends with and learned from the Native Americans who lived near his home. In his later life he fought Indians from time to time to protect his family and other settlers, but he was never the blood thirsty Indian hater that some stories make him out to be. In fact, he often went hunting and fishing with Indian friends up until his old age.

The stories of Daniel Boone were changed to reflect the sensibilities of the times they were written in.

How are some of the stories of America being written today, and do they reflect what actually happened or what we want to believe happened?

Additional Layer

Young kids will enjoy reading *Lewis and Clark: A Prairie Dog For The President*, a short picture book that tells the story of catching a prairie dog to take back to President Jefferson.

On the Web

National Geographic has an interactive map of the Lewis and Clark Expedition you can follow.

http://www.national-geographic.com/lewisandclark/

Famous Folks

Meriwether Lewis and William Clark were the leaders of the Corps of Discovery.

Lewis was a naturalist and his main job was to catalogue the many new species of plants and animals along the way. Clark was the main cartographer for the group, making maps of every place they journeyed.

and a narrow beam. They were shaped sort of like a cigar. Here is a sketch of one of the keel boats that Clark made in his journal:

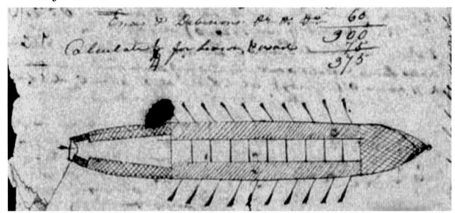

2. Along the way Lewis and Clark were to map the land, find out all they could of the geography and local population from the friendly Native Americans they came across, and take note of plants and animals they found. Prairie dogs, grizzly bears, bighorn sheep, black tail deer, white weasels, and dozens of other new animals and plants were described and drawn in the expedition journals. Many species and descriptions were sent back to Washington D.C. for President Jefferson, including a live prairie dog.

3. They left St. Charles in May of 1804, but it wasn't until October of that year that they reached the Mandan town in North Dakota where they built Fort Mandan and spent the winter. It was here that they picked up a guide and interpreter for the next stretch of their journey. Her name was Sacagawea, a Shoshone woman who knew the country and the languages of the tribes they would be traveling through.

4. The expedition rested at Three Forks Camp, the confluence of three different rivers, for several days while small parties scouted the best route among the rivers. If they chose wrong, they could have to back track and get caught up in the mountains over the winter.

5. They reached the continental divide and Sacagawea's home village where they purchased horses for the next leg of their journey. The mountains were much higher and larger than they expected. There would be no easy water route for trade and travel across the continent like Jefferson had hoped.

6. The company descended, half starving, from the Rocky Mountains through Lolo Pass and to the Nez Perce who fed them and traded dug out canoes for the horses, which were

no longer needed. The Nez Perce told them that the rivers led to a great vast body of water that is not good to taste. They also warned the expedition that the river was rough, not navigable.

7. The Expedition canoed down the river and through the many rapids clear to the mouth of the Columbia River where they build a fort, Fort Clatsop, and spent the wet, rainy winter. The next spring they would travel back, splitting up for part of the journey so as to map more territory.

☻ EXPLORATION: War of 1812

The War of 1812 was one of the least significant of wars ever fought in terms of actual battles, actual lives lost, and immediate goals and outcomes, yet it completely shaped the future of the entire North American continent. The British hardly paid attention to the American war, a mere distraction from the real threat of Napoleon who was invading Moscow in 1812.

Today the British don't even recall that such a war existed. For Americans though, it was a victory, in spite of most of the battles being absolute defeats. The sea battle on Lake Champlain, the bombardment of Baltimore, and the resounding victory at New Orleans gave the little nation pride and patriotism and let the British know that the Americans were serious.

Use the printable set of famous people of the War of 1812 from the end of this unit. Color the person. Cut out on the black rectangle and fold on the gray lines. Write facts or the role of your person in the War of 1812 on the back, upside down to the per-

Additional Layer

The poem "The Star Spangled Banner" was written by Francis Scott Key during the attack on Baltimore in the War of 1812. Learn the story here: http://www.smithsonianmag.com/history/the-story-behind-the-star-spangled-banner-149220970/?no-ist

Take the time to learn the etiquette and words to the national anthem.

Fabulous Fact

The government was forced to abandon Washington D.C. as the British advanced up the Potomac. Dolley Madison (James having joined the army resistance earlier) and her household of slaves and servants saved everything of value they could, including the famous Gilbert portrait of George Washington.

In retaliation for the burning of York, Canada, the British torched nearly all of the government buildings in Washington.

Famous Folks

James Monroe was the fifth president of the United States.

He was wounded during the Revolutionary War, the last American president to have served in that war.

Additional Layer

The Monroe Doctrine directly followed the successful, but perilous, freedom fights led by Simon Bolivar and others in Central and South America. Spain had been kicked out, but for how long? The United States and Britain were both worried.

son so the words will be upside right when the figure is standing on a table. Arrange the folded paper in a triangle shape so the person can stand on a table.

☺ EXPLORATION: Monroe Doctrine

In 1823 President James Monroe gave notice to Europe that the Americas were off limits to European interference and colonization. He warned that America would respond with force, not only on America's behalf, but on the behalf of any nation in the western hemisphere. The policy was intended to allow the newly freed republican Latin American countries time to grow and to prevent European wars from spilling over and unsettling the western hemisphere. Presidents as late as Ronald Reagan have reiterated and invoked the Monroe Doctrine.

This is the key passage from the Monroe Doctrine:

We owe it, therefore, to candor and to the amicable relations existing between the United States and those powers to declare that we should consider any attempt on their part to extend their system to any portion of this hemisphere as dangerous to our peace and safety. With the existing colonies or dependencies of any European power we have not interfered and shall not interfere. But with the Governments who have declared their independence and maintained it, and whose independence we have, on great consideration and on just principles, acknowledged, we could not view any interposition for the purpose of oppressing them, or controlling in any other manner their destiny, by any European power in any other light than as the manifestation of an unfriendly disposition toward the United States.

At the time Monroe issued this proclamation the United States was in no position to enforce it. The army and navy were both small and weak. But the British approved of the Monroe Doctrine, probably as a way to keep the Spanish from interfering with trade in the western hemisphere, and the British navy was strong enough to enforce the peace.

This was the first time that the United States declared its interest in the fate of nations other than its own. It is the opposite of an isolationist policy, and it has been the basic outline of foreign policy for the United States since it was issued.

Some say the U.S. involves itself in foreign nations too often and others say the U.S. has a responsibility to maintain world peace and ensure freedom for as many people as possible. There are all shades of opinions in between.

Think of a modern day example of unrest in some place in the world. Does the unrest threaten the United States directly? Do you think a non-intervention policy would be better or an interventionist response? Why?

Make a poster on a piece of card stock. Write the world problem you have chosen at the top. Then split the rest of the page into two halves. On one half write "non-intervention," and on the other half write "intervention." List reasons for each position and possible consequences. Add illustrations and colors to make your poster interesting.

🙂 🙂 🙂 **EXPLORATION: Slavery in the South**
In early America slavery was legal and common in both the north and south. Wealthy and middle class people owned slaves. A lower middle class family might own just one or two, while a wealthy planter might own hundreds. Slaves were fairly expensive to buy and to keep, though less expensive than a paid servant or laborer.

Slaves were used to replace the labor of the owner with the labor of another. Slaves did all sorts of jobs in early America. They were house servants, nursemaids to small children, field workers, mechanics, wheelwrights, blacksmiths, rope makers, stable boys, seamstresses, cooks, clerks, foremen, doctors, and more.

After the American Revolution the northern states slowly abolished slavery and thousands of slaves were freed. But the South had always had far more slaves than the north because of the plantations, which needed a great deal of labor to make them work. In the late 1700's slavery was even dying out in the South. The farms were based on growing tobacco, indigo, and rice, none of which were especially lucrative by 1800. The plantation owners were downsizing, sometimes giving away or freeing their slaves because they could no longer afford to keep them. But then in 1793 a man named Eli Whitney invented a machine that could automatically remove the seeds from cotton, instead of picking the seeds out one by one by hand. All of a sudden it became profitable for plantations to grow cotton. The South bloomed with cotton fields and southerners bought up slaves again to work the fields.

Some slaves had kind masters who treated them well, but many slaves belonged to brutal masters who beat and abused them verbally and physically for even minor offenses. Whether they belonged to gentle or harsh masters, all slaves were the property of another person and without basic human rights. They could

Additional Layer

The British were absolute masters of the seas and much of the land across the globe from 1815 to 1914. This century of relative peace is known as the Pax Brittanica, Latin for "British Peace." The British served as the world's policemen.

Today the United States has largely taken on the role of global policeman.

Additional Layer

The early 1800's were a time when religious revivals were sweeping the nation. This period was called the Second Great Awakening and was led by Baptist and Methodist ministers. Church membership soared and the revivals also led to the formation of several new churches, including Churches of Christ, The Seventh Day Adventists, the Mormon Church, Christian Church, and the Evangelical Christian church in Canada.

This is an outdoor Methodist camp meeting. People were made to feel guilty and then given a hope for redemption.

Library List

Here are some good books for kids to help them understand slavery in Antebellum America.

Freedom's Fruit by William H. Hooks

The Daring Escape of Ellen Craft by Cathy Moore

The People Could Fly: American Black Folktales by Virginia Hamilton

Minty: A Story of Young Harriet Tubman by Alan Schroeder

To Be A Slave by Julius Lester

A Tale of Two Plantations: Slave Life and Labor in Jamaica and Virginia by Richard S. Dunn

Famous Folks

Eli Whitney invented the cotton gin and set off the American Industrial Revolution.

His invention also had the unintended consequence of cementing slavery in America.

not choose who to marry, where to live, what job to have, what to do with their time, what clothes to wear, who to talk to, and more. If they were beaten, starved, overworked, or abused, there was no law that would protect them.

This is an illustration of the cotton gin from Harper's Weekly. It was published in 1869. In this picture the slaves look happy and content with their lot. What do you think the truth was?

Slave holders by the early 1800's were mostly wealthy plantation owners or townsmen. Most slave owners were white, but there were Native American and black slave owners as well.

The northerners didn't own slaves, but a great deal of the wealth of the north was nevertheless dependent on slavery as the north transported, processed, and manufactured cotton and cotton products in huge quantities. This economic dependence made it very hard politically to get slavery abolished.

Read more about slavery in early America (see the sidebar for book recommendations), then make some background art to use with the slave shadow puppets from the end of this unit. The backgrounds should be scenes of where you might have found a black slave in early America. You could include a cotton field, the interior of a slave cabin, a barn, inside the master's house, a kitchen, or some other place you read about. Place the shadow puppets in front of the scenery pieces while you tell stories of the slaves, sing slave songs, or read more books on slave life.

We used 18"x12" large sheets of construction paper and oil pastels to make our background. You could go way more crafty with colored paper, paint, fabric, and other objects as well. The figures are on card stock.

☺ ☺ ☺ **EXPLORATION: American Indian Wars**

Between 1789 and 1846 forty wars were fought with various native tribes. A loose estimate of 45,000 Native Americans were killed in these conflicts and about 19,000 Americans. The first of the Indian wars with the new United States was instigated by the British, who still hoped to reclaim North America. The tribes were defeated, their lands taken, and most of them escaped north to Canada. Other tribes moved further west.

Other wars were the result of American settlements pushing westward. In these wars the natives would often have victories, but never for long. Eventually the overwhelming firepower and resolve of the Americans would win out. Defeated tribes were forced to make treaties, giving up their lands. Some were forcibly removed without even the formality of war, the natives complying resentfully rather than perishing. Some tribes, like the Blackhawk, fought back, but eventually they too were moved westward.

South, in Florida, the Seminole Indians were repeatedly attacked, and they attacked back in turn. Eventually the constant importunities from settlers and reports of natives on the war path convinced Andrew Jackson, who had become president in 1829, to call for a permanent removal of all southeastern Indian tribes east of the Mississippi.

West of the Mississippi regions that had been settled early by

Additional Layer

Most American slaves were devout Christians. Many of them saw the teachings of Christ as solace and hope that even if freedom eluded them in this life, they would have it in the next.

The story of Moses, who freed the Israelites from Egyptian slavery inspired them as well.

This site talks about Negro Spirituals, religious songs sung by slaves.

http://www.negrospirituals.com/index.html

The spirituals give insight into the belief system of the slaves.

Additional Layer

Children of slave women adopted the status of their mothers, a reversal of common law. Why was American law rewritten and what were the consequences? Why does the law normally require fathers to acknowledge and care for their children?

How did slavery affect families in other ways?

Fabulous Fact

In 1832 the Supreme Court ruled the Cherokee had limited sovereignty under the Federal Government in Worcester vs. Georgia, which would have protected their boundaries from the encroachments by the states who the court ruled had no legal rights on native lands. President Andrew Jackson famously defied the court's 1832 ruling, stripped the Cherokee of all their rights (both legal and as humans), treated them as a conquered nation, and used the army to force them off their land in favor of white settlers. He said, "John Marshall has made his decision; now let him enforce it! ... Build a fire under them. When it gets hot enough, they'll go."

Writer's Workshop

Andrew Jackson was popular among the people in the U.S. because of his status as a war hero during the War of 1812. His behavior otherwise was often ruthless and high handed.

Read more, then write a newspaper editorial to convince people to either vote for or against Andrew Jackson as president.

Americans were already experiencing Indian wars, including Oregon Territory, California, Utah, Texas, and New Mexico. The wars in the west would continue until the late 1800's with a few conflicts arising after 1900. We will learn more about the Indian Wars in the west in Unit 4-6.

Research an Indian war. We recommend one of these, unless you have a particular reason to learn about another:

- Cherokee-American Wars
- Second Seminole War
- Northwest Indian War
- Creek War
- Black Hawk War

After you have learned more about the war you chose, make a Native American war bonnet. Make a headband out of construction paper and add paper "feathers." On each feather write a fact about the war. Give an oral presentation to a group.

Older kids (6th or 7th grade and up) should also write a paper describing the events of the war, notable individuals involved in the war, causes and effects of the war, and the student's opinion of the war.

☺ ☻ ☻ EXPLORATION: Trail of Tears

The Trail of Tears was the forced relocation of several Indian tribes from their homes in the southeast United States to Oklahoma Territory. In all, approximately 46,000 people were forcibly removed from their homes and escorted 1,000 miles west by U.S. military troops.

The Five Civilized Tribes - the Choctaw, Cherokee, Seminole, Creek, and Chickasaw - had adopted many of the cultural traditions of the white people who had emigrated to the New World. They lived in houses built of boards, went to church in Christian churches, wore western clothing, sent their kids to school where they learned English and math and history. They worked as blacksmiths, farmers, school teachers, and lawyers, and owned black slaves like other southerners. But they were also legally autonomous nations living within the borders of Florida, Mississippi, Georgia, North Carolina, Tennessee, and Alabama. As more and more white settlers moved to these states, the government was continually pressured to give the valuable Indian lands to the states and send the Indians way out west to land that nobody wanted.

Finally in 1830, Andrew Jackson signed the Indian Removal Act, which gave the president the power to negotiate treaties with the tribes which would take their lands in exchange for land in the west. Using strong arm tactics, including armed invasions and deceit, and in spite of protests and legal battles, the people were removed from their homes by force. Along the trail thousands died due to hardship, exposure, exertion, privation, disease, and physical attacks, all while under the "protection" of the army. Old men, little children, pregnant women, the sick, the handicapped, all traveled west with inadequate food and clothing on their own two feet.

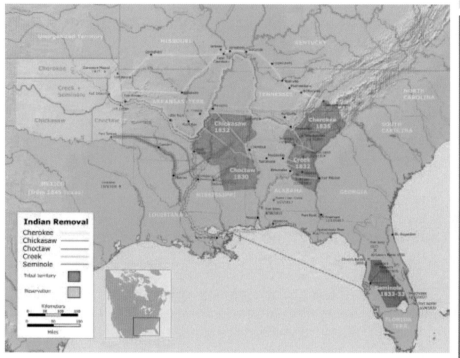

One of those who was forced west was George W. Harkins, a Choctaw. His people had decided after massive pressure and deliberation to voluntarily remove themselves, signing a treaty and turning over their land to the U.S. Government in exchange for land in Oklahoma. He wrote an open letter to the American people which was widely reprinted in newspapers across the country.

Read the letter here: http://www.ushistory.org/documents/harkins.htm.

While there certainly were greedy and evil people who desired the removal of the Native Americans, many, many Americans were appalled and distressed by the turn of events in their land of liberty and rights. Among these were Davy Crockett, Daniel Webster, and Henry Clay, who all spoke out in behalf of the Cherokee and other nations' rights.

On the Web

This 16 minute video argues that the Trail of Tears should never have happened based on morality and legality.

https://www.youtube.com/watch?v=qalhDKL-rWEQ

Additional Layer

Major Ethan Allen Hitchcock who found the remains of the American soldiers after the Dade Massacre said "The government is in the wrong, and this is the chief cause of the persevering opposition of the Indians, who have nobly defended their country against our attempt to enforce a fraudulent treaty. The natives used every means to avoid a war, but were forced into it by the tyranny of our government."

The Seminole Indians had been tricked or forced into signing a treaty. When they refused to honor it, the Americans waged total war on their people.

Teaching Tip

Don't lose the opportunity of taking the ethical lessons learned in this unit and applying them to your kids' lives and modern politics.

Deep Thoughts

America doesn't always live up to her ideals of personal freedom, free markets, hard work, respect for the rights of individuals, and the rule of law. Why do people say one thing and then do another?

But sometimes America is truly good. Think of an example.

Famous Folks

John Ross was the top tribal leader of the Cherokee at the time of the Indian Removal Act.

Legend says that his wife gave up her blanket to a cold child on the trail and, in doing so, lost her own life. She is buried in an unmarked grave somewhere along the way.

Alexis de Toqueville, the celebrated Frenchman who observed American life, witnessed the removal of some of the people and said,

In the whole scene there was an air of ruin and destruction, something which betrayed a final and irrevocable adieu; one couldn't watch without feeling one's heart wrung. The Indians were tranquil, but sombre and taciturn. There was one who could speak English and of whom I asked why the Chactas were leaving their country. "To be free," he answered, could never get any other reason out of him. We … watch the expulsion … of one of the most celebrated and ancient American peoples.

Several basic principles were offended that led to the tragedy of the Trail of Tears.

1. First, the white settlers were covetous, which means they wanted someone else's stuff so badly they would hurt those people to get it.
2. The white settlers were under the impression that the Indians were not equal to them and did not deserve equal protection nor equal rights.
3. Property rights were not respected, which led to great suffering and loss of life, since property is needed to sustain life.
4. The government failed in its duty to protect its citizens and instead used force to conquer and oppress them. The rule of law failed as the President overrode the supreme court decisions and the states refused to submit to the federal government rulings and decisions.

Make a paper plate mobile to represent the Trail of Tears.

At the end of this unit you will find a printable template of tears, each one printed with a word representing a principle that, if followed, would have prevented the tragedy.

Talk with your kids about how these principles apply to their treatment of people in their daily lives as well as how they apply to us as a nation.

☺ ☻ EXPLORATION: War With Mexico

Mexico was suffering from repeated Indian raids from the north, and to buffer this they encouraged the settlement of Americans in the Texas Territory. The Texans, though, did not like the autocratic governance of Mexico and revolted. They won their independence after some setbacks like the Battle of the Alamo. Mexico never recognized Texan independence, so when the U.S. annexed Texas in 1845 Mexico was annoyed. Cross words were exchanged, and then the United States invaded quickly, taking three quarters of Mexico and capturing Mexico City. A treaty ending the conflict gave the United States Texas, California, Arizona, New Mexico and all the land northward. Very little of this land was inhabited by Mexicans, but it was increasingly being settled by Americans. Mexico got $15 million and debt forgiveness.

Sentiments about the war were sharply divided along partisan lines. Pro-slave Democrats favored it because it could add slave holding territory. Whigs opposed it because they thought it was an unjust war waged for greedy purposes and would give slave holders more power. Opposition to the war and his refusal to pay taxes supporting it landed Henry David Thoreau in jail and inspired him to pen "Civil Disobedience."

Read the Wikipedia article about the Mexican American war at https://en.wikipedia.org/wiki/Mexican%E2%80%93American_War, then make a map of the newly acquired territory. Draw the outline free hand, using a map from the Wikipedia article as a reference. You can place a few of the major cities and forts on for reference points. Texture color code each section of the map by placing rough surfaces under it and doing a crayon rubbing

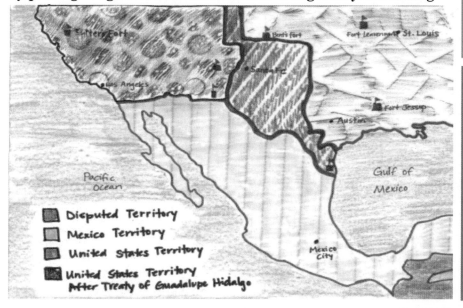

Famous Folks

Alexis de Toqueville was a French soldier who had served under General Washington during the Revolutionary War. He came back to America later in his life to observe the new republic and see if this experimental form of government was working. He wrote about it in "Democracy in America."

On the Web

Read this eye witness account of the Battle of the Alamo: http://www.eyewitnesstohistory.com/alamo.htm.

Famous Folks

Here are some other famous people from this time period who you should check out.

Davy Crockett
Jim Bowie
Sam Huston
Washington Irving
Ralph Waldo Emerson
Samuel F.B. Morse

GEOGRAPHY: PACIFIC STATES

Fabulous Fact

This is a NASA image showing the Cascade Range.

To the west, along the coast, the land is lush and green. But the mountains create a rain shadow and the land to the east is much drier.

Look up "rain shadow" in a dictionary or online.

Additional Layer

Silicon Valley is the nickname given to the Santa Clara Valley, just south of San Francisco. It is the world capital for tech innovators including Apple, Ebay, Facebook, Cisco, Intel, and more.

California, Oregon, Alaska, and Washington are all on the west coast of North America. Hawaii is located about 2,500 miles southwest of California in the middle of the Pacific Ocean. The climate of Hawaii and the western portion of the Pacific states is wetter and the temperature more moderate because of the influence of the ocean.

Just along the coast, running from the north to the south, is a range of tall mountains that block rain from reaching the eastern portion of the states and causing the rain to fall more heavily to the west. This creates temperate rain forests in Washington and Oregon, leaving the eastern sides of these states very dry.

This is the city of San Francisco, California with the famous Golden Gate bridge in the foreground. The coastal states have some very large cities like Seattle, Portland, Los Angeles, and San Diego.

The early settlers to Oregon, Washington, California, and Alaska came from the east looking for land, gold, or timber. Many came west in huge wagon trains across the central plains and deserts. Others came in ships on a months long dangerous journey around the horn of South America from Boston, New York, or another eastern port. The west coast was settled earlier in general than the center of the country and still has a much larger population than the central states today.

Hawaii has a unique history among American states. It was inhabited by Polynesian people and discovered by Europeans in 1778. The British armed King Kamehameha with modern guns, and Kamehameha united the islands into one kingdom though conquest. The British and French began to fight over possession of the islands, so in 1874 Hawaii declared it would trade exclusively with the Americans.

American businessmen flooded into the islands establishing pineapple, sugar cane, coffee, and cattle farms. Soon they were very powerful, and on January 17, 1893 they overthrew the Hawaiian monarchy. Washington D.C. feebly protested. Grover Cleveland, the president at the time, vehemently objected, but the congress refused to commit troops, and so nothing was done. Cleveland's successor, William McKinley, was an expansionist; he enthusiastically annexed Hawaii officially as a territory of the United States in 1900. Hawaii became a state after WWII as a step toward independence, because as a territory they had no voice in the United States government.

☺ ☺ EXPLORATION: Timeline of West Coast History
Make an illustrated timeline on a long sheet of freezer paper.

- 1805 Lewis and Clark arrived on the west coast in Oregon
- 1812-1840 Fur trade at its height
- 1819 U.S. acquired Spanish claims to the northwest
- 1821 Mexico gained the territory of California from Spain
- 1830's Christian missions established in the Pacific Northwest
- 1836 The Oregon Trail was established
- 1843 The Great Migration; thousands of families headed for the Willamette Valley in Oregon
- 1844 The California Wagon Trail was established
- 1846 American settlers, supported by Mexican Californios, seized the garrison fort at Sonoma and raised the Bear Flag over the new Republic of California
- 1848 California became a territory of the U.S. after the U.S. won the war with Mexico
- 1849 California Gold Rush began
- 1850 California became a U.S. State
- 1850-1860 Several massacres of native populations by militias; death by disease of natives caused rapid population decreases
- 1853 Seattle was settled as a lumber and trading town
- 1858 U.S. Army defeated the northwest tribes for the final time
- 1859 Oregon became a state
- 1869 Transcontinental Railroad finished, linked east to west
- 1889 Washington became a state
- 1890's-1920's California was a leader in the political Pro-

Additional Layer

In 1820 Protestant Christian missionaries arrived from England and the United States, and in a few decades nearly all of Hawaii had become Christian.

The missionaries didn't just preach. They also preserved the histories, tales, and language of Hawaii by writing it down for the first time.

Teaching Tip

The maps and other explorations in this section can be added to a dedicated portfolio or scrapbook focused on the states.

Every other unit throughout Year Four is a study of the states in a particular region. Each state will have a map activity and many will have fun printables or activities that can be combined into a personal portfolio.

Famous Folks

Herbert Hoover, Richard Nixon, Ronald Reagan, and Earl Warren are all famous political figures from California.

On the Web

San Diego has an amazing zoo. Visit it online.

http://www.sandiego-zoo.org/

The zoo is very involved in conservation efforts.

Additional Layer

Books that take place in California include:

Island of the Blue Dolphins

The Grapes of Wrath

Esperanza Rising

The Ballad of Lucy Whipple

Al Capone Does My Shirts

The Circuit: Stories From the Life of a Migrant Child

By the Great Horn Spoon

Kildee House

California Politics

Some major political issues in the state of California include fights over water rights, immigration laws, balancing the state budget, gerrymandered districts, property taxes and property values, and gun rights.

gressive movement
- 1926 Route 66 was built, creating a major highway from the east into California
- 1930's Major dam projects built along the Columbia and other rivers all over the northwest to provide power
- 1955 Disneyland opened in Anaheim
- 1965 Watt's Riots in Los Angeles over race relations
- 1980 Mt. St. Helens erupted

☺ ☺ EXPLORATION: Elevation Map of California

Label a map of California including the major landmarks and cities from your student atlas. Then color it as an elevation map, with the high mountains dark brown, the lower mountains and foothills light brown, the plains and coastal areas light green, and the areas below sea level dark green.

You can find a printable California map at the end of this unit. All of the state maps are also available as free printables at http://www.layers-of-learning.com/geography/.

☺ ☺ ☺ EXPLORATION: California Facts

Here are some facts about California. Read each one and talk about it, looking up pictures online as you go. You can add drawings around your map of California to show the state symbols and add some of the landmarks. You could also draw them into a passport book (see right sidebar).

- Tree: Redwood
- Flower: California Poppy
- Motto: Eureka
- Nickname: Golden State
- Bird: California Quail
- Capital: Sacramento
- Large Cities: San Francisco, Los Angeles, San Diego
- Song: I Love You California

- Major Industries: Farming vegetables and fruits, entertainment, tourism, technology, mining
- Largest religions: Catholic, The Church of Jesus Christ of Latter-day Saints, Baptist, other Christian denominations
- Landmarks: Golden Gate Bridge, Death Valley, Sequoia National Park, Lake Tahoe, Sierra Nevada Mountains, Coastal Ranges, Sacramento River, San Joaquin River, Colorado River, Sonoran Desert, Pacific Ocean

☻ ☻ ☻ **EXPLORATION: Californian Farms**

California is a major producer of food for North America and beyond. Almonds, walnuts, avocados, tomatoes, eggs, chickens, cilantro, celery, lettuce, plums, olives, grapes, corn, and many other crops are grown in all regions of the state. Check out this agriculture map of California and learn about some of the foods that grow there: http://kids.cfaitc. org/wgo/geography/. Explore the rest of the site for lots more about California agriculture.

Then make a Californian farm art project. Start by drawing farm fields separated by roads on a piece of white or light brown card stock. Then fill in each field section with rows of green, yellow fields, or rows of trees. We used a combination of oil pastels, colored pencils, paints, and permanent markers. After the paint has dried write the name of each California crop in its field section and give the page a title.

☻ ☻ **EXPLORATION: Oregon Population Map**

Color a map of Oregon (see the printables at the end of this unit)

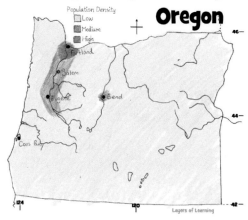

showing the population density. Keep it simple, using three colors. The darkest shade is the most populated area. The medium shade is used to show the next most populated area. Then the rest of the state is all colored in the lightest shade. Make a key.

Additional Layer

Oregon's state nickname is the "Beaver State" because of the beaver fur trade that was important in its history. Find out more about the fur trade and why it ended.

The back of the Oregon flag has a beaver on it.

Oregon is the only state with a two sided flag.

Additional Layer

The Pacific Northwest has been a center for the environmental movement since the beginning. Learn more about this history.

Additional Layer

Learn more about lighthouses, which dot the rugged and beautiful Oregon coast. Some of them are still active.

This is the Heceta Head Lighthouse.

Photo by John Fowler, CC license, Wikimedia.

☺ ☺ EXPLORATION: Oregon Fact Flip Page

Make a flap fact sheet about Oregon using the printable from the end of this unit. The printable includes covers to go on each section of flip facts.

There are tabs to tape on to sheets about famous people, a pocket to slide animal fact cards into, a timeline to mark up, a cover for pages about landmarks, and a cover featuring the Oregon map for pages about state symbols. You will need to trim your own pages to size to fit under the covers for each section.

Glue or tape each of the elements to a piece of card stock.

☺ ☺ ☺ EXPLORATION: Washington Map

Label and color a map of Washington State. You can find a map of Washington at the end of this unit.

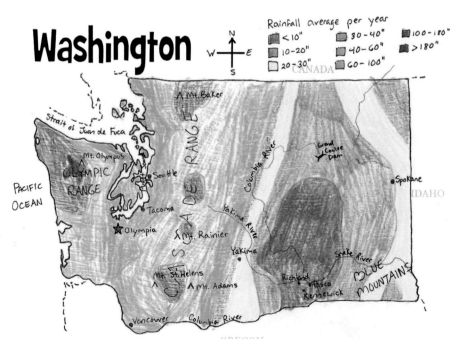

Here are some places to label:

Mt. Olympus
Mt. Rainier
Mt. St. Helens
Mt. Adams
Mt. Baker
Cascade Range
Blue Mountains
Olympic Range

Seattle
Spokane
Tacoma
Olympia
Vancouver
Yakima
Pasco
Kennewick
Richland

Columbia River
Yakima River
Snake River
Puget Sound
Pacific Ocean
Grand Coulee Dam
Strait of Juan de Fuca

Then color the map to show precipitation. Washington State is interesting in its precipitation patterns because it is easy to see how the ocean and the mountains direct where the rain will fall. Washington has both deserts and rain forests in the same state. You can find average annual rainfall information in a student atlas or online.

☺ ☻ **EXPLORATION: Washington Facts**
Draw a large apple tree on a sheet of paper. Print the Washington State Apple Facts worksheet from the end of this unit on to red paper and cut out each apple (or color the apples after they are printed). Glue the apple facts to your tree as you read them together.

☺ ☻ **EXPLORATION: Hawaiian Alphabet**
There are only 12 letters in the Hawaiian alphabet and five of those are vowels, making Hawaiian a very melodic and beautiful spoken language. (a, e, i, o, u, k, m, w, n, l, h, p) Every letter is pronounced, even when two vowels are right next door to each other. Hawai'i, for example is pronounced "Ha-wa-ee". The w has a slight v sound to it, somewhere between a v and a w, unless it is at the beginning of the word.

Learn some words in Hawaiian:

Aloha = hello, goodbye, love
Mele Kalikimaka = Merry Christmas
Ohana = family
Keiki = child
Mahalo = thank you
Kane = man
Wahine = woman
Hale = house

☺ ☻ ☻ **EXPLORATION: Map of Hawaii**
Hawaii is made up of 8 main islands: Oahu, Hawaii, Kauai,

Teaching Tip
State Studies are excellent topics for lap books. A lap book begins with a file folder and kids add in flaps, pockets, and flip-open pages filled with facts, images, reports, maps, and so on.

On The Web
For more about some specific topics on Washington and Pacific Northwest history check out this: http://www.washington.edu/uwired/outreach/cspn/Website/Classroom%20Materials/Curriculum%20Packets/Curriculum%20Packets.html.

Writer's Workshop
Choose a famous person, event or place in Washington and write a report.

Some ideas:
• Mt. St. Helens eruption
• Discovery of the Strait of Juan de Fuca
• Whitman Mission
• Construction of Grand Coulee Dam
• History of Seattle
• Bill Gates and the founding of Microsoft

Make it interesting by turning it into a project like one of these: http://www.layers-of-learning.com/karens-big-list-of-book-projects/.

Fabulous Fact

Every branch of the military: Army, Air Force, Marines, Navy, and Coast Guard, has major bases in Hawaii. About 1/3 of the Hawaiian economy is based on the needs of the military.

Fabulous Fact

The island of Kauai is one of the wettest places on earth. It rains nearly every day and is very lush and green. Its nickname is the "Garden Isle."

Photo by Frank Kovalchek, CC

Additional Layer

The state motto is: "Ua mau ke ea o ka aina I ka pono" which means "The life of the land is perpetuated in righteousness."

If you were to choose a motto for yourself or your family, what would it be?

Maui, Niihau, Molokai, Lanai, and Kahoolawe, but the entire archipelago has over 130 islands and stretches 1,600 miles.

Use your student atlas and the printable Hawaii map from the end of this unit to make a resource map of Hawaii. Draw little icons for fishing, tourism, trade, sugarcane, pineapple, coffee, and military.

☺ ☺ ☻ EXPLORATION: Snorkeling

The most popular sports in the islands are ocean sports. The water is warm year round. In the winter the waves on the north shore are truly stupendous, and surfing and body boarding reign. In the summer the waves die down and snorkeling is in season. Dive under the waves when you make this underwater Hawaiian fish scene. Research some of the fish that swim in the Hawaiian waters and paint or draw them onto a piece of card stock. Let the painting dry, then make a frame for the painting shaped like a snorkeling mask.

Here are some fish to consider: humuhumunukunukuapua'a, Fisher's Angelfish, Japanese Angelfish, Moana kali, combtooth blenny, chevron butterfly fish, Hawaiian spotted cardinal fish, Hawaiian Dascyllus, White eel, and flying fish, plus many more. You might also see sea turtles, dolphins, whales, and other marine animals.

☺ ☺ ☻ EXPLORATION: Surfing For Facts

Learn some facts about Hawaii and write them in the surfboard outline. You'll find a template of a short board in the printables at the end of this unit. Search for facts online or in books about Hawaii.

☺ ☺ ☺ **EXPLORATION: Alaska Map**

Use a student atlas to label and color the major cities and landmarks of Alaska. Use the printable map from the end of this unit.

☺ ☺ ☺ **EXPLORATION: Mush!**

Make an Alaskan sled dog team. You'll find printable sled dogs at the end of this unit. Color the dogs, cut out each one, and fold along the top to make a dog that can stand up. On the one side of each dog write a fact about Alaska. You can complete it as you read a book about Alaska.

☺ ☺ ☺ **EXPLORATION: Big Map**

In Unit 4-1 we started a big map project of the United States. If you don't have the big map from Unit 4-1, you can print a map in any size you like from this site: http://www.yourchildlearns.com/megamaps/print-usa-maps.html.

Earlier you should have labeled and colored the oceans and seas surrounding the United States. During this unit you should label each of the Pacific States.

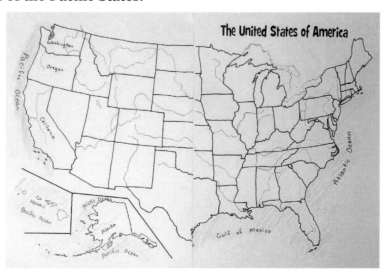

Writer's Workshop

This is a Heiau on Kauai.

A Heiau is a sacred site where Hawaiians used to perform human sacrifices and other forms of worship. Their religion was brought to the islands by conquering Fijians. The religion prior to the invasion was much gentler.

Write a story or poem based around a Heiau.

Fabulous Fact

In 1890 gold rush fever hit Alaska. The population boomed, but it wasn't until black gold was discovered that Alaska was considered stable enough to become a state.

Additional Layer

Alaskan natives belong to several different tribal groups including Inuit, Yupik, Aleut, Haida, Tlingit, Eyak, Athabaskan, and Tsimshian.

Learn more about one of these tribes, their traditions and culture.

SCIENCE: MOTORS & ENGINES

Additional Layer

Think about how technology has changed the social structure and economic mobility for millions.

People of even modest means used to have servants to help them do work. The servants were, of course, on the bottom of the social scale. Today even wealthy people rarely have servants. Instead we have washing machines, automobiles, dishwashers, microwaves, and a thousand other machines, big and small, to help us do our work. Fewer people are needed for drudgery and more can develop their minds and talents.

Famous Folks

Michael Faraday was an English scientist who hated math, but loved experimentation. We have him to thank for our modern electric lifestyle.

Often people want to change energy into motion so a machine can do our work for us. Machines do work that we couldn't do, and they tend to do it much faster and more precisely than we could ever do it. Complex machines, like an engine, are made up of simpler machines like inclined planes, gears, pulleys, and levers. Engines convert energy into motion.

☺ ☺ EXPERIMENT: Build an Electric Motor

This activity shows how electrical energy can be turned into motion. This is the principle upon which all motors work.

You will need:

- A battery holder for a C or D size battery
- A battery to go in your holder
- A flat bar magnet
- Copper wire, enamel coated, 22 gauge or thicker, and about 3 feet long
- Two large size, uncoated paper clips or stiff, uncoated copper wire (18 gauge). Rubbing paper clips or wire down with steel wool will ensure that any coating is removed.

Use instructions from this website: http://sci-toys.com/scitoys/scitoys/electro/electro.html.

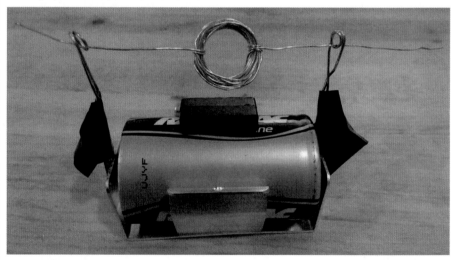

Or you can buy a small DC motor kit from Home Science Tools for about $8.

Once you have built an electric motor, either from scratch or from a kit, you can experiment with it. Here are some ideas.

- Change the number of magnets, the type of magnet, or the direction of the magnets.

- Try different gauge or lengths of wire for your electromagnet coil.
- Try different types or numbers of batteries.

☺ ☺ ☺ **EXPERIMENT: Dissect an Electric Motor**

If you have an old broken fan, hair dryer, kitchen mixer, RC car, electric toothbrush, or something else with an electric motor, take it apart (remove from the power source first) to see how everything fits together to make the engine run. Can you identify all the parts? Maybe you can even fix it so it will run again.

☺ **EXPERIMENT: Faraday's Law**

Faraday's Law says that an electric current can create a magnetic field and, conversely, a changing magnetic field can create an electric current. This was a huge leap forward in scientific understanding, to link magnetism with electricity made possible motors, electric generators, and transformers. Modern life is based on this concept, which you become acutely aware of if ever your power goes out.

The voltage created by a moving magnetic field is equal to the change in magnetic flux (the strength of the magnetic field) divided by the change in time. This can be shown as a mathematical equation:

$$E = \Delta B / \Delta t$$

E stands for Electromotive Force (we now say voltage instead). This symbol, Δ, is the Greek letter delta. Mathematicians and scientists use it to mean "change in." B stands for magnetic flux and t stands for time in seconds.

The real key in this relationship between magnetism and electricity is that there must be motion to convert from one to the other.

When Faraday was working on his discovery he made a device that included passing an electromagnet through a coil of wire and measuring the current produced with a galvanometer.

You can set up the same experiment to show how a

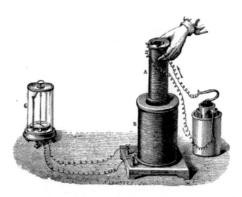

This is Faraday's apparatus to test magnetic induction. The cylinder to the right is a battery hooked up to a coil of wire to make an electromagnet. The cylinder on the far left is a galvanometer to measure electric current.

Additional Layer

To help kids understand how important motors are to modern life, go on a tour around your home and identify the motors around you.

They are in vacuum cleaners, electric trains, RC cars, hair dryers, fans, refrigerators, microwaves, washing machines, computers, dishwashers, electric toothbrushes, and dozens of other machines, both small and large.

How would life be different if motors had never been invented?

On the Web

This site has a great explanation of how motors work for middle grades and up. http://www.explainthatstuff.com/electricmotors.html

Have your kids read this and take notes on what they learned. The notes should include at least one labeled diagram or drawing and the basics of how an engine works.

On the Web

This short video explains how an electric DC motor works.

https://www.youtube.com/watch?v=LAtPHA-NEfQo

Vocabulary

- Dynamo
- Magnet
- Coil
- Electric
- Armature
- Magnetic field
- Rotor
- Electromagnet

Famous Folks

Thomas Newcomen, an English ironmonger and Baptist lay preacher, invented the first commercially viable steam engine. It was used to pump water out of tin and coal mines in Cornwall, which in the late 1700's, had been delved deep enough to begin filling with ground water.

This is Newcomen's steam engine for pumping water out of mines.

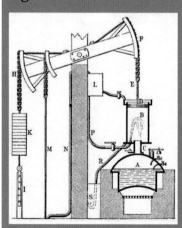

Writer's Workshop

Write about what it would be like to live in a world without motors and engines.

magnet passing through a coil of wire produces an electric current. You will need a coil of wire, a bar magnet and a multimeter. Your set up should look like this:

Now test these things by checking the read out on the multimeter:

1. Magnet at rest.
2. Magnet moved toward the coil.
3. Magnet stationary inside or very near the coil.
4. Magnet moving away from the coil.
5. Magnet moving slowly in and out of the coil versus moving quickly in and out of the coil.

☻ ☻ EXPEDITION: Tour a Power Plant

Start by watching this video: https://www.youtube.com/watch?v=0ftl-WM6wms.

Draw and label a picture showing the way that electricity is generated.

All power plants use coils of wire and magnets to produce electricity. The motion needed to move the coil of wire around the magnet comes from the flowing river in the case of hydroelectric power, the blowing wind in the case of a windmill, or heated and expanding steam in the case of a nuclear or coal powered plant.

Tour an actual power plant near you.

☻ ☻ EXPLORATION: History of the Engine

Read up on the history of the steam engine or the internal combustion engine, how it was invented, and the different types of engines through history.

Make a book to show off what you have learned. At the

end of this unit is a printable outline of a steam locomotive that you can use as a shape book for the steam engine and a printable outline of an automobile that you can use for a shape book about the internal combustion engine. Cut out as many pages as you need of the outline and staple them together on one edge.

☺ ☺ **EXPERIMENT: Pop Can Hero Steam Engine**
The first engines invented used steam to move the parts. The first steam engine was invented in 1698 by Thomas Savery. Other men, such as Thomas Newcomen and James Watt, improved the design until it became truly useful in the mid 1800's. Steam engines continued to be the most popular type of engine until the early 1900's when they were replaced by diesel powered engines. Steam engines have been used to power trains, automobiles, boats, and mills. Steam power is still used to produce electrical energy across the world.

Steam engines on a train have a fire box in which wood or coal is burned. The heat from the fire causes water in pipes from a tank to boil. As the water boils, it produces steam. The steam is inside an enclosed space and, as a gas, it wants to expand as it is heated, causing pressure to build up. The pressure is then used to move pistons which are attached to rods, which are attached to wheels.

This project shows how steam creates pressure that causes movement. You will need:

- Aluminum soda pop can, unopened
- Small nail
- Tea light candles
- String

1. With the nail, carefully punch a hole in the side of the unopened pop can, about halfway up and drain out all of the soda. Punch a hole on the exact opposite side as well. Rinse the can out by putting water in through the opening and draining it again.
2. Put water into the can so it has an inch or two in the bottom of the can. Use the

Famous Folks
James Watt was a Scottish inventor and chemist who was fascinated with the Newcomen steam engine. He improved the design to make it radically more efficient and introduced rotary motion, meaning it could power something other than a water pump. It is Watt's engine that powered the Industrial Revolution.

Fabulous Fact
Steam engines are external combustion engines while the engines in modern automobiles are internal combustion engines.

In an external combustion engine the fire (combustion) is outside the container where the steam is expanding.

In an internal combustion engine the expanding fluid is in the same container as the combustion.

Some steam power is produced without combustion like in a solar or nuclear powered engine.

Additional Layer

Get a small demonstration model to experiment with how gears work to yield more result using less energy. I got a simple model online for less than $10.00. My kids (ages 6 and 8) can follow the instructions on their own to build over 30 different things using gears.

Photo by Blue Plover, CC license, Wikimedia.

Additional Layers

Learn hands-on mechanics. Changing a flat tire, checking the oil and other basic fluids, and filling a car with gas are good places to start. As kids get older they can learn to change brakes, wipers, oil, and other mechanics.

On the Web

If you want to make a science fair worthy engine project out of household stuff, try the instructions from this seven year old.

http://steamsciproj. blogspot.com/

nails to dent the can a bit at the holes so that the steam, when it comes out, will be directed in a clockwise direction and make the can spin.

3. Carefully bend the pop tab up without popping the top open. Tie a string to the tab and hang the can above some tea candles so the can is able to turn freely.

4. Light the candles and wait for the water to heat. Once the water is heated and steam builds up, the steam will shoot out of the holes you have made and make the can spin.

Chemical energy (the burning candle) is transformed into mechanical energy (the spinning can). This is the basic principle upon which all steam engines work.

☺ ☺ ☺ **EXPLORATION: Color the Engine by Number**
Color the picture of the engine, which you will find in the printables at the end of this unit. The engine you're coloring is for an automobile. Each part of the engine is numbered and a color is assigned to each number. Learn about the parts as you color.

This is a very simplified four cylinder engine. Besides the basic piston assembly, engines also have alternators to charge the battery and run electrical equipment like the radio, fans to cool the engine, belts and pumps to move water, complicated transmission boxes, brake assemblies, and complicated computer systems that monitor and run parts of the engine.

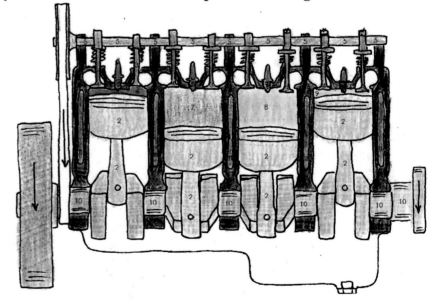

☺ ☺ ☺ **EXPLORATION: Dissect a Gas Engine**
Go to a lawn mower repair shop and ask if they have any old lawn mower motors lying around. Your kids can take it apart, learn about all the parts, watch it work, and play with it.

Use a guide to learn the names of the parts and what each one does. An owner's manual usually lists the part names.

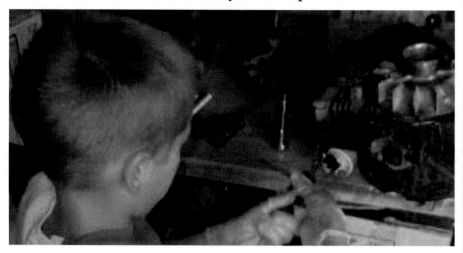

By the end of the lesson my kids could tell about each part of the engine, describe how each part functions, and talk about how the pieces work cooperatively. A hands-on project like this taught them so much more than any other engine lesson could've.

☺ EXPLORATION: The Brayton Cycle

George Brayton was an American engineer who worked on gas engines and developed an engine cycle that could produce a constant pressure, rather than a rhythmic one as we find in most gas engines. The Brayton Cycle, named after him, is the principle upon which turbine engines and jet engines are based. First the air is compressed, then it is ignited, and finally the great heat and pressure dramatically increase the volume of the air, which drives the engine. Watch this video, which does an admirable job explaining the function of a jet engine: https://www.youtube.com/watch?v=LolwC_Bytz0.

Finally, use this page from NASA to help you draw and label your own diagram of the parts of a jet engine and how they work: https://www.grc.nasa.gov/www/k-12/UEET/StudentSite/engines.html.

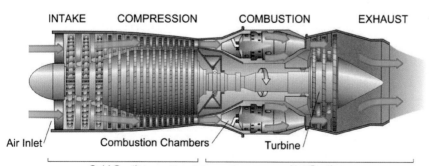

INTAKE   COMPRESSION   COMBUSTION   EXHAUST

Air Inlet   Combustion Chambers   Turbine

Image by Jeff Dahl, CC license, Wikimedia

Additional Layer

Research what kinds of engines are the most efficient, especially in the vehicle industry.

On the Web

Here is a 4 minute video that shows the internal parts of a combustion engine and how it works:

https://www.youtube.com/watch?v=DKF5d-Ko_r_Y

This video is a lot more detailed and 32 minutes long. In it, Eric the Car Guy dissects a real engine and shows off the parts.

https://www.youtube.com/watch?v=saP-GX-1qC4M

Fabulous Fact

In a gas engine, the fuel/air mixture is lighted with a spark from the spark plug. But in a diesel engine pressure is used to create heat which ignites the fuel without need for a spark. Remember what happens to temperature when pressure is increased?

This is a glow plug. It is used to increase the heat in the chamber until the engine is warm enough to maintain combustion.

THE ARTS: TALL TALES

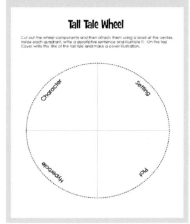

The American frontier was a scary, dangerous place. Wild animals, vast lands, inhospitable deserts, dense forestland, and towering mountains made for a challenging life for early Americans. This was the time of tall tales. They began as stories told and retold on the American frontier, and the best ones spread far and wide and were eventually written down. Telling tales was a form of entertainment on the frontier, so the storytellers didn't hold back; they set the stories in familiar settings, but made the characters larger than life and the tasks even larger.

Pecos Bill Lassos A Tornado. By Maroonbeard, CC BY-SA 3.0 , via Wikimedia Commons

☺ ☺ ☺ EXPLORATION: Elements of a Tall Tale

Tall tales have characters, a setting, and a plot that are distinct to their genre.

1. Characters - They are extreme, with exaggerated talents, qualities, and skills. Often they were based on real people, but then exaggerated beyond belief.

2. Setting - The settings of tall tales were based on the audience. Generally, they were set in early America, but more specifically, the railroad men told tales of railroad men like John Henry, the cowboys told tales of cowboys like Pecos Bill, and lumberjacks told stories of lumberjacks like Paul Bunyan. The exact scenario was contrived to be most entertaining to the audiences who listened to them.

3. Plot - Like the characters, the plot of a tall tale was often based on true things, but then stretched quite a bit until it

was no longer true. It's kind of like a fisherman's fish stories. A fisherman may catch an impressive two foot fish, but with each telling the fish gets bigger and stronger until the fisherman has caught an unbelievable 15 foot shark.

Use the "What Makes A Tall Tale?" printable as you read through some of the tall tales in this unit. Fill one out for each tale and then bind them all into a booklet together. You can use the boxes for both words and illustrations about the elements of each tale. See the next exploration to help you fill out the hyperbole boxes.

☺ ☻ EXPLORATION: A List of Hyperboles A Mile Long

Hyperbole is extreme exaggeration. It is an embellishment used to entertain and make a point. Here are a few examples:

- If I don't eat something right now, I'll die.
- Gail is as skinny as a toothpick.
- Great grandpa is older than dirt.
- He knows everything about science.
- Don't touch my new bike; it cost a bazillion dollars.
- She was in such a hurry that she just broke the land speed record.
- You need an elevator to look him in the eye.

Write ten of your own hyperboles. They can be humorous and as unbelievable as you like.

As you read through the tales in this unit keep a hyperbole log called "A List of Hyperboles A Mile Long." Of course, your list won't really be a mile long, but then, that's the whole idea of exaggerating. You'll find a printable one to use in the printables section. Write down and illustrate the hyperbole in the box, then check the applicable boxes near each entry.

☺ ☻ EXPLORATION: Johnny Appleseed

Johnny Appleseed's real name was John and he really did plant lots of apple trees, make orchards, and sell apples. He was kind to people and animals alike and respected living things. Read the story of Johnny Appleseed, and try to separate fact from fiction. We aren't really sure exactly which details of the story are true. Did he really keep a wolf as a pet? Did he wear a pot on his head as a hat? Did he really put out campfires so as not to harm insects? How many apple trees did he really plant throughout his lifetime?

Write "Dear John" letters on your own stamped stationary so you can ask Johnny which of the parts of his story are true.

Famous Folks

Jim Bridger was a mountain man. He was a scout, a trapper, and a guide in the American frontier. He was part owner of the Rocky Mountain Fur Company, was one of the first European Americans to see the Great Salt Lake and geysers of Yellowstone, and built Ft. Bridger. As much as he is known for these accomplishments, he is also known as a great storyteller, one of the early tellers of tall tales.

Writer's Workshop

Imagine that you are Johnny Appleseed. You are about to head out on the open road into the vast wilderness. You're all on your own and all you have is what you can take with you in the backpack on your back. Choose seven items you would take that could fit in your pack. Write about them and why you chose to take each one.

Tall Tales Checklist

- The story is full of exaggerations.
- The main character has superhuman abilities.
- The problem is larger than life.
- The plot is funny and full of action.
- The main character overcomes.

On The Web

Although Davy didn't really wear one, we still think of him when we see a coonskin cap. Check out this website if you want to try your hand at crafting your own:

http://www.coonskin-cap.com/pioneer.htm

1. Cut an apple in half. Use a paintbrush to paint on the open face of the apple.
2. Stamp the apple down, leaving a print on the paper. Create a border at the top and bottom of your page to make an apple border.
3. Once you've finished with a color, wipe the paint off of the apple using a paper towel and repeat using whatever colors you'd like.
4. Use a small paintbrush to add in the stem and leaf details, then let your painting dry.
5. When the page is dry, cut it out and glue it to a colorful background sheet.
6. Write a letter to Johnny asking all about his apple seed adventures.

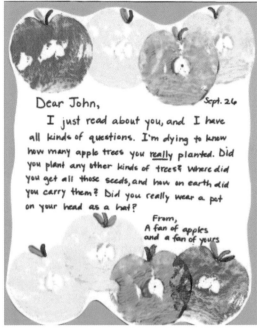

Dear John,   Sept. 26

I just read about you, and I have all kinds of questions. I'm dying to know how many apple trees you really planted. Did you plant any other kinds of trees? Where did you get all those seeds, and how on earth did you carry them? Did you really wear a pot on your head as a hat?

From,
A fan of apples
and a fan of yours

☺ ☺ ☺ **EXPLORATION: Davy Crockett, The Coonskin Congressman**

It's pretty unlikely that Davy Crockett killed a bear when he was only three years old, but he was a folk hero nonetheless. He was

actually a politician, serving as the representative from Tennessee in the U.S. House of Representatives. He later moved to Texas where he died fighting at the Alamo.

David, himself, was quite the storyteller. He loved to spread tall tales about himself. They say he first introduced himself to Congress by saying, "I am that same Davy Crockett, fresh from the back woods, half-horse, half-alligator, a little touched with the snapping turtle. . . I can whip my weight in wildcats. . .

and eat any man opposed to Jackson." He loved to tell tales to entertain his Washington friends.

Read about Davy Crockett. Now pretend you are running against Davy Crockett for the position of Congressman from Tennessee. Make a campaign poster with your own larger than life accomplishments and qualities. What would it take to one up the great storyteller, Davy Crockett?

☻ ☻ ☻ **EXPLORATION: Sally Ann Thunder Ann Whirlwind**

Sally Ann Thunder Ann Whirlwind was supposedly the wife of Davy Crockett. In reality he was married twice, but never to anyone named Sally.

Read the story of the amazing Sally Ann, full of spunk and tough as nails. Notice all of the bragging that goes on in tall tales.

Write a brag speech about yourself. Begin by making three lists:

1. Talents and skills you wish you had.

2. Possessions you wish you had

3. Feats you wish you had accomplished.

These can be impossible and fantastical. Use your three lists to write a brag speech about yourself, tall tale style. Deliver the speech to an audience.

☻ ☻ **EXPLORATION: Paul Bunyan**

Unlike some of the other folk heroes, nothing about Paul Bunyan is true. He is definitely a larger than life character and one of the most famous tall tale heroes.

While reading about Paul Bunyan, keep a record of the location of each of his accomplishments on a map of the United States. Sketch an outline map of the mainland United States. Draw a little scene at each spot and caption it with what he did. Here are some you might include:

- He was born in Maine, and nearly exhausted the five storks who delivered him.
- He slept in a cradle off the coast of Maine, sinking seven warships who tried to awaken him. The waves made by his cradle rocking still fill the Bay of Fundy.
- He built Niagara Falls so he could take a shower when he was just two years old.
- He made the Mississippi River when one of his water wagons

Memorization Station

Born on a mountaintop in Tennessee,

Greenest state in the land of the free.

Raised in the woods so he knew every tree,

Kilt him a b'ar when he was only three.

Davy, Davy Crockett, King of the wild frontier.

-Theme song from the Disney Version of Davy Crockett

Additional Layer

Paul Bunyan symbolizes might and strength, the willingness to work hard, and the resolve to overcome any obstacles in your path. All of these were honored values of the founders, settlers, and frontiersmen of early America.

Famous Folks

Samuel Clemens, aka Mark Twain, was a master of the literary tall tale. He could weave a story with the best of them and seemed to make even the most ordinary situations seem extraordinary. Better yet, he made them extraordinarily funny.

Writer's Workshop

"Paul's clothing was so large they had to use wagon wheels for buttons. They used a lumber wagon drawn by a team of oxen as a baby carriage. When he outgrew this his parents put him on a raft off the coast of Maine."

Take this quote and turn it on its head. Rewrite it for a teeny tiny person instead of giant Paul Bunyan.

leaked.

- Paul cleared every tree in the Dakotas, making way for the Midwestern farmland of America.
- He dug the Great Lakes so his ox, Babe, could have a watering hole.

- He piled up rocks and made Pike's Peak.
- When he cried, his saltwater tears formed the Great Salt Lake.
- Babe, his big blue ox, was trying to dig out a field mouse and dug out Mammoth Caves instead.
- Paul missed snow while he was in the southeast, so he invented cotton.
- Paul invented golf when he was hitting rocks from the southern tip of Texas to the Florida panhandle.
- While searching for firewood, Paul dragged his heavy axe and carved out the Grand Canyon.
- Paul and Babe trekked through Minnesota leaving footprints that would become Ten Thousand Lakes.
- Paul put out his campfire with a pile of rocks one day, and we still call that pile Mt. Hood.
- He dug out the Puget Sound during a contest with Billy Puget, then threw some dirt back in to show Billy a thing or two. And that's where the San Juan Islands came from.
- When Babe passed away Paul cried so hard that his tears formed the Missouri River.

☺ ☺ ☻ EXPLORATION: John Henry

Many tall tales originally took the form of songs, and John Henry has perhaps the most famous songs of the tall tale genre. Lots of versions of his story have been written in song, from ballads to work songs. Here is one version of *The Ballad of John Henry*: https://youtu.be/OF-3t8Id6mA.

John Henry was a real steel driver who helped carved tunnels and set rails for the railroads, though a lot of the details of his life are disputed. The story goes that the steel driving workers were going to be replaced by a steam powered hammer, but that John Henry had a race with the machine and won. He fame was made even more secure when he died at the close of the competition with his huge hammer in his hand.

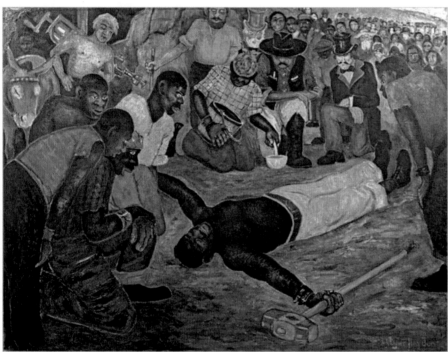

John Henry Lies Dead After beating the Steam Drill. Picture from the Smithsonian American Art Museum, via Wikimedia Commons

Watch this version of the story called *John Henry and the Railroad, The True Tall Tale*: https://youtu.be/j3LVFdWBHVM.

One of the often overlooked elements of tall tales is that they depicted the character traits that were most valued by early Americans. Discuss the values John Henry had. What kind of a man was he? Did his values determine his success? How does this relate to the American dream?

☺ ☺ ☻ EXPLORATION: Pecos Bill

They say Pecos Bill rolled out of his family's covered wagon without anyone noticing, and then was raised by a pack of coyotes.

On The Web

Here is a printable fill in the blank hyperbole story:

http://www.education.com/worksheet/article/hyperbole-story/

Additional Layer

John Henry's story wasn't the only man versus machine railroad event. In 1827 the first U.S. railroad company, the Baltimore and Ohio Railroad, didn't have a reliable steam engine. They relied on horse drawn trains because they were better at traversing the rough terrain. Peter Cooper designed an engine called Tom Thumb. A challenge ensued between the Tom Thumb steamer and a horse drawn engine. The steam engine quickly pulled away from the horse drawn one, but then broke a belt and had to stop, leaving the horse drawn engine to cross over the finish line first. Cooper's steam engine drew attention anyway though, and it was soon in production. Although it lost the challenge, the machine was clearly much quicker and stronger than the horse drawn versions.

Additional Layer

Some scholars say that some of these tall tales are actually fakelore, not folklore. Fakelore doesn't mean the story has fake elements, since in fact, folklore is known for its fake elements. Rather, fakelore means stories that were written to mimic the actual oral tales told by early Americans, but that were not genuinely traditional. Advertisers have especially been known to invent larger than life characters to promote things. Paul Bunyan and Pecos Bill have both been called fakelore.

Fabulous Fact

Keelboats were big, flat bottomed boats that were used to carry things down rivers like the Mississippi. They had no motors. They were piloted using long poles that steered them down the river.

This is an Alfred Waud engraving of a flatboat full of passengers in the late 1800's.

He grew up to become a cowboy, using a rattlesnake as a lasso. He lassoed a twister once, ate dynamite, and shot all the stars from the sky except one. Read some stories about Pecos Bill. Choose one of these projects:

- Write your own storybook version of Pecos Bill, with a chapter for each new adventure. Use "cowboy language."
- Tall tale heroes like Pecos Bill have permeated books, poems, songs, comic books, plays, and movies. Write your own version of one of these that features Pecos Bill.
- Make a "Missing Person" poster including a description of Pecos Bill, where he was last seen, and what to expect if you find him.
- Write a diary entry as though you were Bill's mother or father when you discovered he was lost from your wagon.
- Compare Pecos Bill with another of the tall tale heroes using a Venn diagram. Do they share common virtues? Abilities? Accomplishments? In what ways are they different?

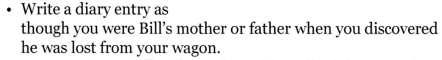 **EXPLORATION: Flatboat Annie**

Annie Christmas was called Flatboat Annie because she was the pilot of a flatboat on the Mississippi River. Traditionally, this was a job only men held, but Flatboat Annie was not traditional by any definition. She was tough and strong and could outdo the other keelboat captains. Along with the standard tall tale character traits, she also had a fair bit more compassion than some of the others. She showed that being tough, rugged, and independent does not mean you must be unkind.

Make a foldable using the printable from the end of the unit. Cut along the lines to create little doors that open up. Write your answers to each question inside the doors. Under the title door, draw a picture of how you envision Flatboat Annie.

EXPLORATION: Tall Tale Heroes Book of Stamps

The U.S. Post Office issued a special set of postage stamps honoring American folk heroes in 1996. It included stamps that featured Paul Bunyan, John Henry, Pecos Bill, and Casey at the Bat. Design and create your own set of stamps based on your favorite tall tale heroes. You can use the printable postage stamp template from Layers of Learning.

http://www.layers-of-learning.com/design-a-postage-stamp/

☺ ☻ ☻ **EXPLORATION: Super Heroes, Modern Tall Tales**
Choose your favorite tall tale hero and your favorite modern day superhero. Discuss the idea that superhero stories are modern tall tales. Here are a few talking points:

- List the traits and characteristics of the superhero you chose and the tall tale character you chose. Do they have anything in common?
- Are there any major differences between our modern superhero stories and the tall tales of early America?
- Do you think the genres serve a similar purpose culturally?
- What do the traits of the heroes say about our values?
- Can you think of what a superhero in early America might have looked like and accomplished?
- What might a tall tale character in modern America accomplish?
- Do television and movies tell a different story than would've been told in an oral storytelling culture like frontier America?

☺ ☻ ☻ **EXPLORATION: Your Own Tall Neighborhood**
Write a tall tale about your neighborhood, city, state, or region and one or more of its features. Begin by brainstroming some things that are unique or interesting about the area you live. Create a tale that tells how those things came to be.

For example, I live just down the street from a very little lake tucked into the mountains. My tale could tell about how the lake used to cover almost the whole state of Idaho until a friendly ogre wandered out of a mountain cave and drank most of it up. Now the lake is named after that thirsty ogre.

For this exploration, feel free to create a tall tale hero if you'd like, but focus more on the setting and how something from your area may have originated in an exaggerated way.

☺ ☻ ☻ **EXPLORATION: I'm Awfully Tall Myself**
Illustrate yourself as a tall tale character. First, make a list of ten qualities you possess in your real life. These could include what you look like, your favorite things, talents, hobbies, habits, and character traits.

Additional Layer

Use an atlas with a map of the U.S.A. to spot the location of each tale you've read.

Additional Layer

Want to read more tall tales? Here are some more famous heroes that have great tales:

Slue-foot Sue
Annie Oakley
Mike Fink
Calamity Jane
Thunder Rose
Casey Jones
Febold Feboldson
Old Stormalong

Writer's Workshop

Choose a character from one of the tall tales you've read during this unit. Now imagine he or she is your parent. What is the best part about having this character as your mom or dad? The worst? How do people treat you differently because of it? What traits would you hope to inherit from your character?

Additional Layer

In the early 1900's tall tale postcards became popular. Crafty photographers manipulated images that showed oversized fruits, fish, and other products on the postcards. This helped perpetuate the idea that American was a land of plenty and encouraged growth and settlement.

Learn more about these trick postcards and view a few of them:

http://www.amusing-planet.com/2010/11/tall-tale-postcards-of-twentieth.html

Create your own tall tale postcard either by using creative photo editing or by hand drawing.

Try to feature your own state or region with a creative postcard. Whether you draw it by hand or take a photo and edit it, you can have it printed at a photo center postcard style. You can even actually mail it to someone.

Now think about ways you can exaggerate those qualities. For example, if you are short, you might become no taller than a carton of milk. If you are a good friend you might say you are such a good friend that you had no less than a crowd of thirty clamoring to be by your side at any given time. Make sure to include both physical attributes that even a stranger could see and also character traits that someone could know only by getting to know you.

Make an illustration of what you would look like as a tall tale character. Surround your picture with captions that describe your attributes in tall tale style.

If you want to, you can turn your page over and write about an adventure you might have as a tall tale character.

☺ ☺ ☺ EXPLORATION: Literal Tall Tales
Now you're going to write your own tall tale.

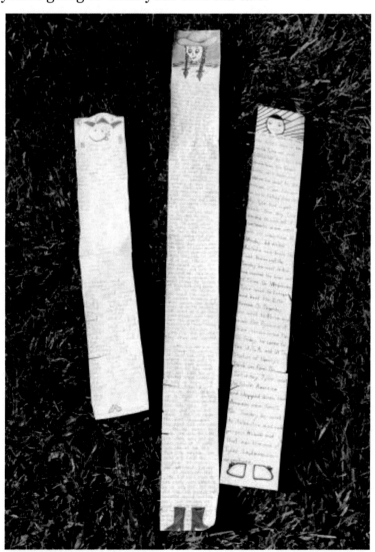

Begin by thinking of a character who has some special qualities and abilities. Write down as many as you can think of. Next, write a list of ten things your character might say. This will help you begin to think like your character, and whether or not you actually use the dialogue in your story, it will come through in your story. Now think of an everyday event or task, like going grocery shopping or playing a game of soccer. Next, add in some unbelievable events. Use at least three amazing feats and include lots of adjectives. Make sure to throw in hyperboles whenever you have a chance. Impossible exaggerations are really what make a tall tale, so use lots of them. End your tall tale with one final unbelievable event. Make it your biggest exaggeration of all.

Now use the printable template at the end of this unit to write your story on. You can print out extras if you've written a really long whopper, and then just tape the extra columns together for an extra tall tale. Draw your character's head at the top and feet at the bottom, so the tale is making up the body. Write out the entire tale going down the page.

Share your really tall tale with an audience.

Additional Layer

Have a discussion comparing tall tales with literature from other cultures, times, or places. Describe some similarities and differences between these and tall tales. You might consider including fairy tales, fables, Greek myths, and science fiction stories.

Teaching Tip

Depending on your kid, you might want to accompany this lesson with one about lying. What is the difference between lying and telling a tall tale? If you are clear that the story isn't true, there's nothing wrong with telling a fun story, but you shouldn't stretch the truth or tell untrue tales as the truth.

Coming up next . . .

Unit 4-3

Industrial Revolution
US Landscapes - Energy
Romantic Art I

My Ideas For This Unit:

Title: _____   **Topic:** _____

_____
_____
_____
_____
_____
_____
_____
_____
_____
_____

Title: _____   **Topic:** _____

_____
_____
_____
_____
_____
_____
_____
_____
_____

Title: _____   **Topic:** _____

_____
_____
_____
_____
_____
_____
_____
_____
_____

My Ideas For This Unit:

My Ideas For This Unit:

Title: _____   **Topic:** _____

_____

_____

_____

_____

_____

_____

_____

_____

_____

_____

_____

Title: _____   **Topic:** _____

_____

_____

_____

_____

_____

_____

_____

_____

_____

_____

_____

Title: _____   **Topic:** _____

_____

_____

_____

_____

_____

_____

_____

_____

_____

_____

Daniel Boone

This is Daniel Boone and his wife Rebecca. They were early settlers who crossed the Appalachian Mountains and blazed a trail into the Kentucky Country. So many stories have been told and exaggerated about Daniel Boone that he became a legend. The Boones are examples of the American ideals of resourcefulness, bravery, honesty, and hard work.

Timeline Unit 4-2: Expanding Nation

1787 4-2
Northwest Ordinance allows white settlement in areas formerly owned by Native American tribes who had sided with the British during the Revolution

1787-1795 4-2
Northwest Indian War

1795 4-2
Treaty of Greenville deprives twelve northwest Native American nations of their lands

1803 4-2
Louisiana Purchase

1804 4-2
End of slavery north of the Mason-Dixon line

1805 4-2
Lewis & Clark Expedition reaches the Pacific

1808 4-2
Slave trade becomes illegal in American and British law

1812-1814 4-2
War of 1812

Aug 1814 4-2
British burn Washington D.C., including the White House

1818 4-2
War against the Seminoles in Florida

1818 4-2
Treaty between U.S. and Britain makes the 49th parallel the border between U.S. and Canada in the west

1819 4-2
Spain gives Florida to the U.S.

1820 4-2
Settlers reach the Mississippi

1821 4-2
There are now 23 states

1823 4-2
Monroe Doctrine issued

1829 4-2
Andrew Jackson is president

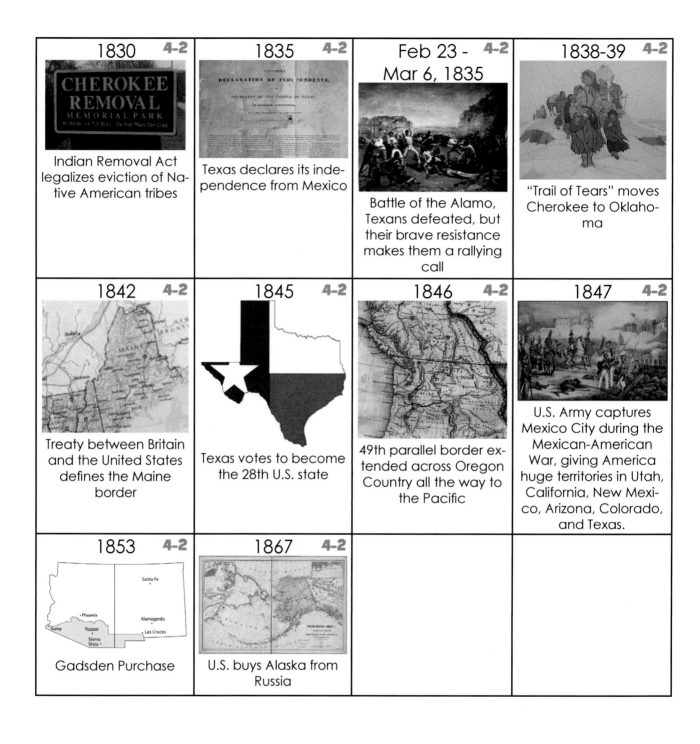

1830 **4-2**	1835 **4-2**	Feb 23 - **4-2** Mar 6, 1835	1838-39 **4-2**
Indian Removal Act legalizes eviction of Native American tribes	Texas declares its independence from Mexico	Battle of the Alamo, Texans defeated, but their brave resistance makes them a rallying call	"Trail of Tears" moves Cherokee to Oklahoma
1842 4-2	**1845 4-2**	**1846 4-2**	**1847 4-2**
Treaty between Britain and the United States defines the Maine border	Texas votes to become the 28th U.S. state	49th parallel border extended across Oregon Country all the way to the Pacific	U.S. Army captures Mexico City during the Mexican-American War, giving America huge territories in Utah, California, New Mexico, Arizona, Colorado, and Texas.
1853 4-2	**1867 4-2**		
Gadsden Purchase	U.S. buys Alaska from Russia		

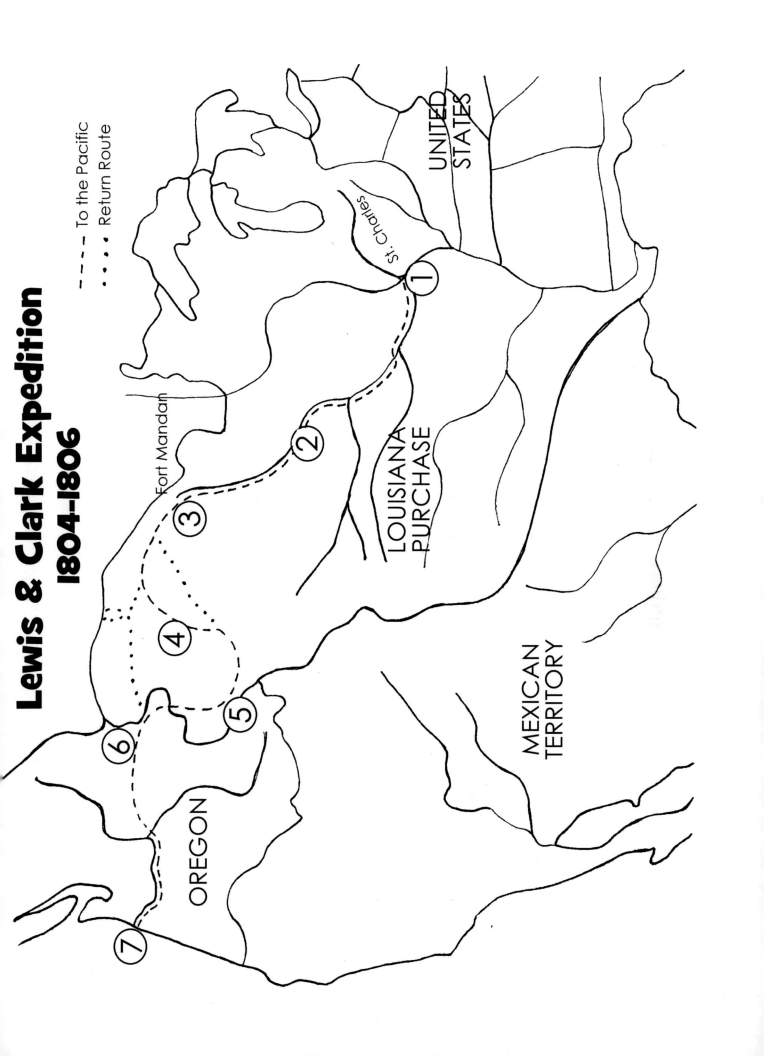

Lewis & Clark Expedition
1804-1806

- - - To the Pacific
· · · · Return Route

UNITED STATES

St. Charles

LOUISIANA PURCHASE

Fort Mandan

MEXICAN TERRITORY

OREGON

1 2 3 4 5 6 7

War of 1812 Figures

Laura Secord

William Henry Harrison

Isaac Brock

James Madison

Andrew Jackson

Tecumseh

Slave Silhouettes

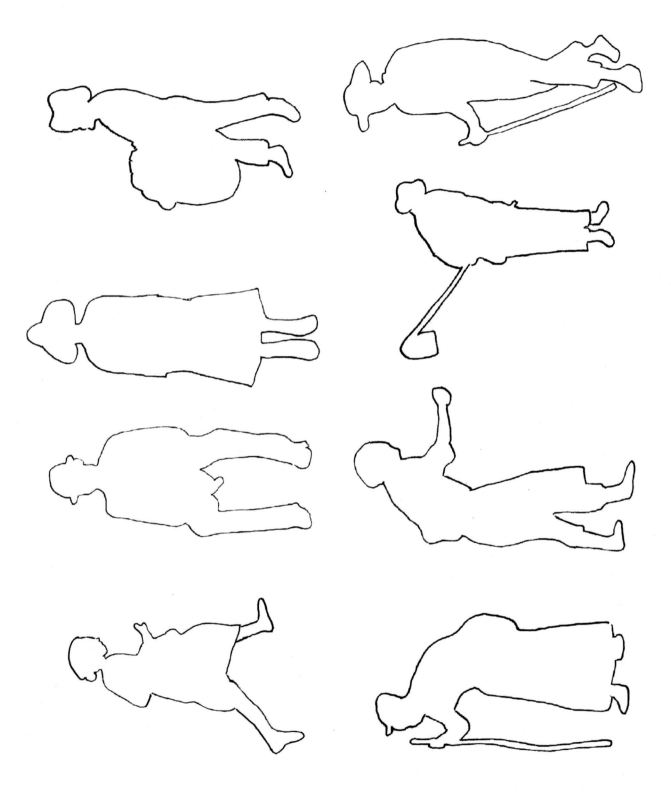

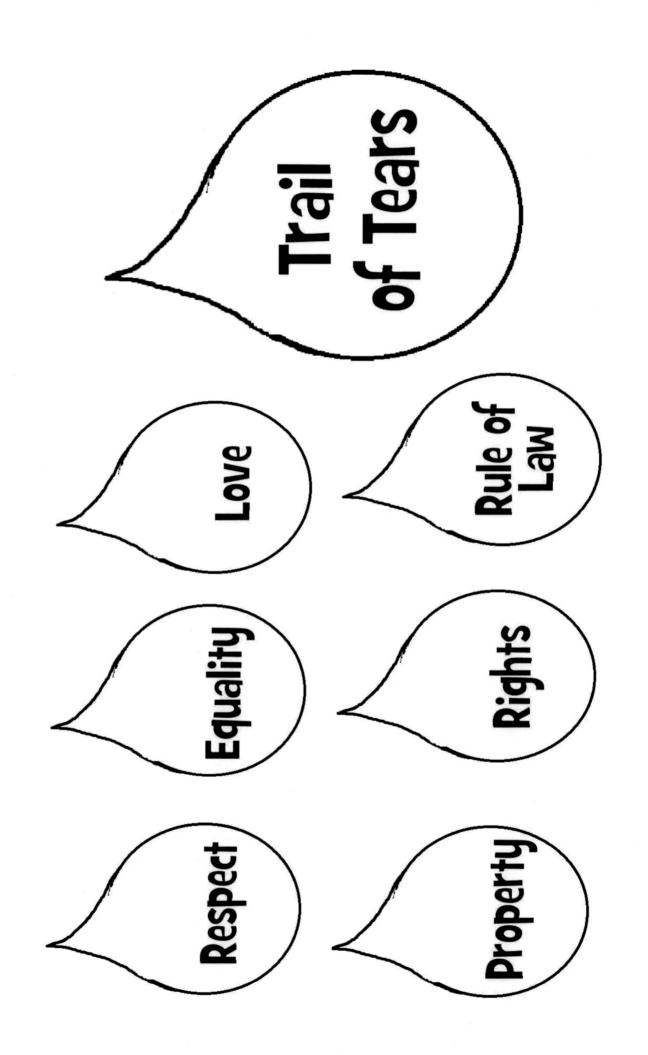

California

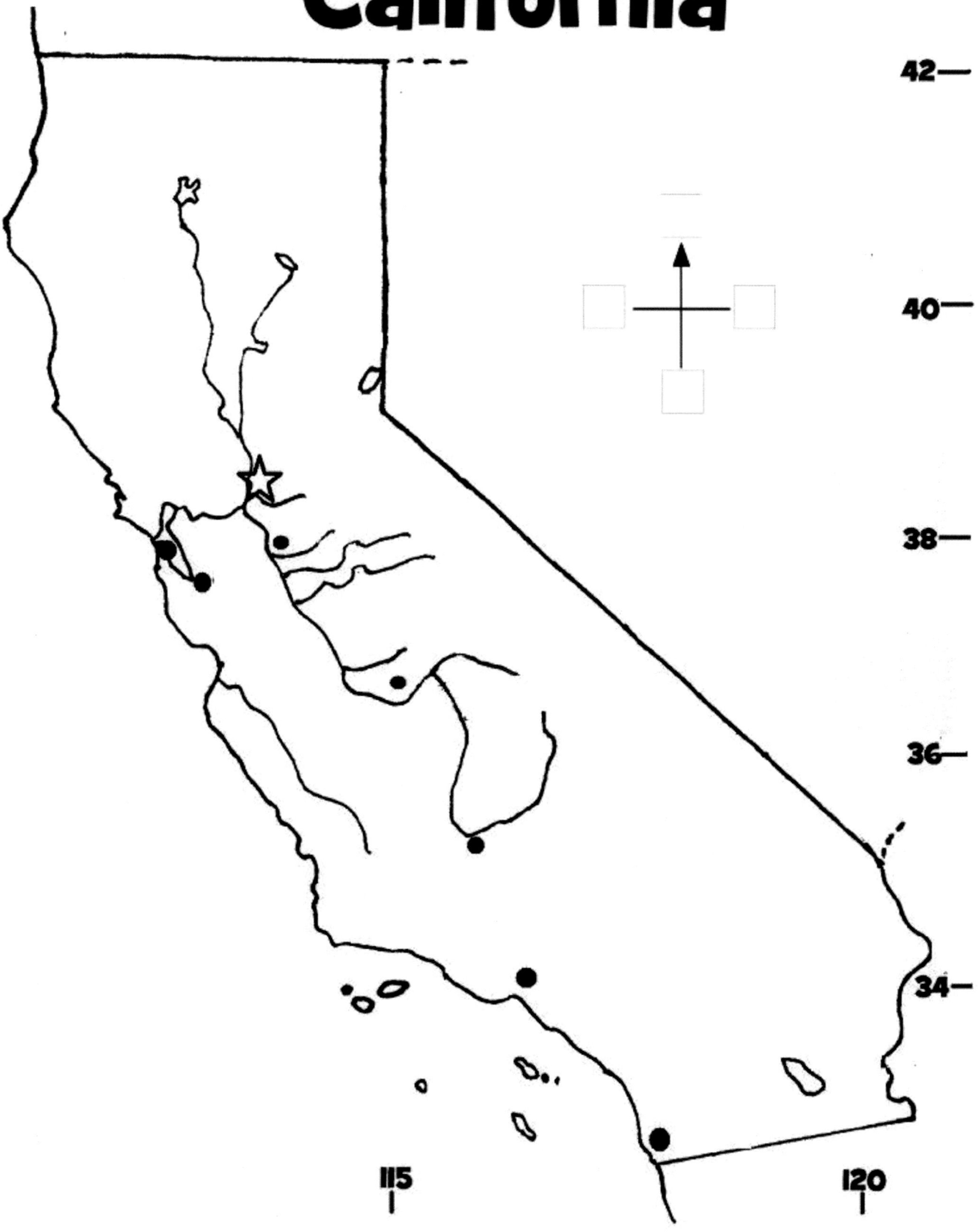

42—

40—

38—

36—

34—

115

120

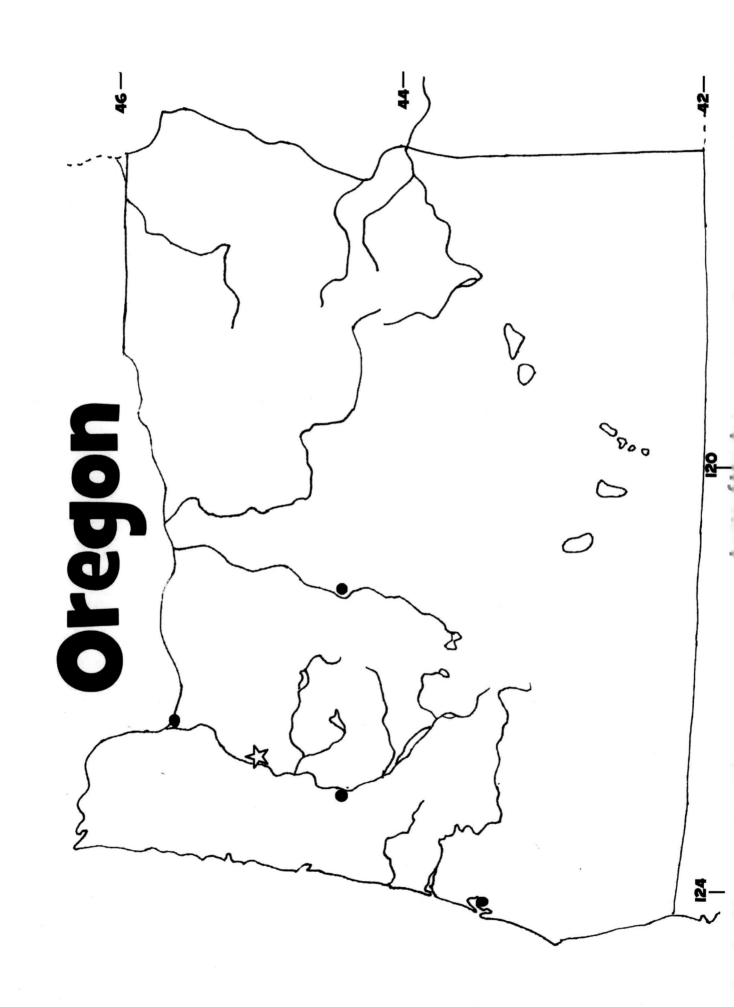

Oregon

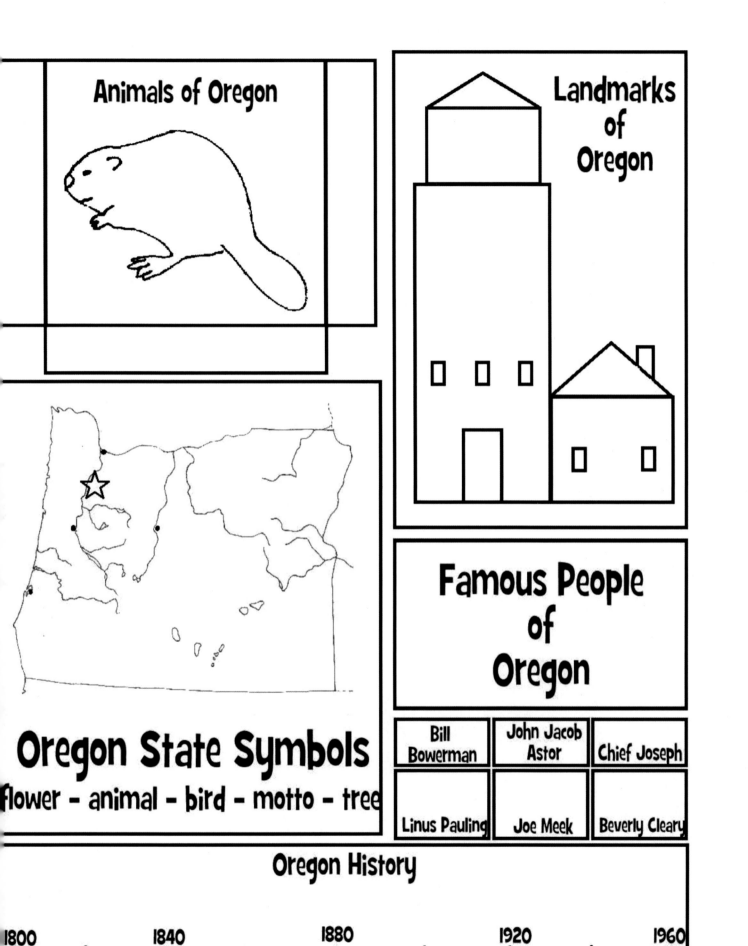

Animals of Oregon

Landmarks of Oregon

Oregon State Symbols
flower - animal - bird - motto - tree

Famous People of Oregon

Bill Bowerman	John Jacob Astor	Chief Joseph
Linus Pauling	Joe Meek	Beverly Cleary

Oregon History

1800	1840	1880	1920	1960

Washington

CANADA

IDAHO

OREGON

Washington State Apple Facts

Washington has over 1000 dams and gets almost all its power from hydroelectric sources.

The capital is at Olympia, south of Seattle.

The state flower is the Coast Rhododendron.

Grand Coulee Dam is the largest dam in the United States, producing 21 billion kilowatt hours of electricity every year, supplying nine western states and part of Canada with power, and it currently (no pun intended) only runs at half capacity.

The Space Needle is a famous landmark.

Spokane in the eastern side of the state is the second largest city in Washington.

Washington, the 42nd, became a state in 1889.

Washington is nicknamed "The Evergreen State"

The state was named after George Washington.

Washington is the largest producer of apples in the United States.

The state motto is Al-Ki, a Chinook word which means by and by, or hope for the future.

Washington's native tribes include Chinook, Nisqually, Quinault, Puyallup, Cayuse, Colville, Spokane, and Nez Percé.

Hawaii

Niihau

Kauai

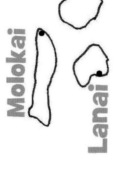

Oahu

Molokai

Lanai

Maui

Kahoolawe

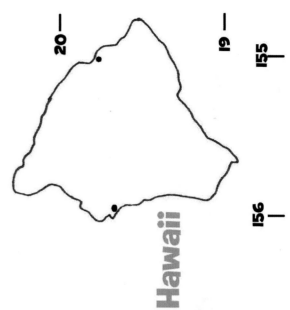

Hawaii

160   159   158   157   156   155

19   20   21   22

Hawaii

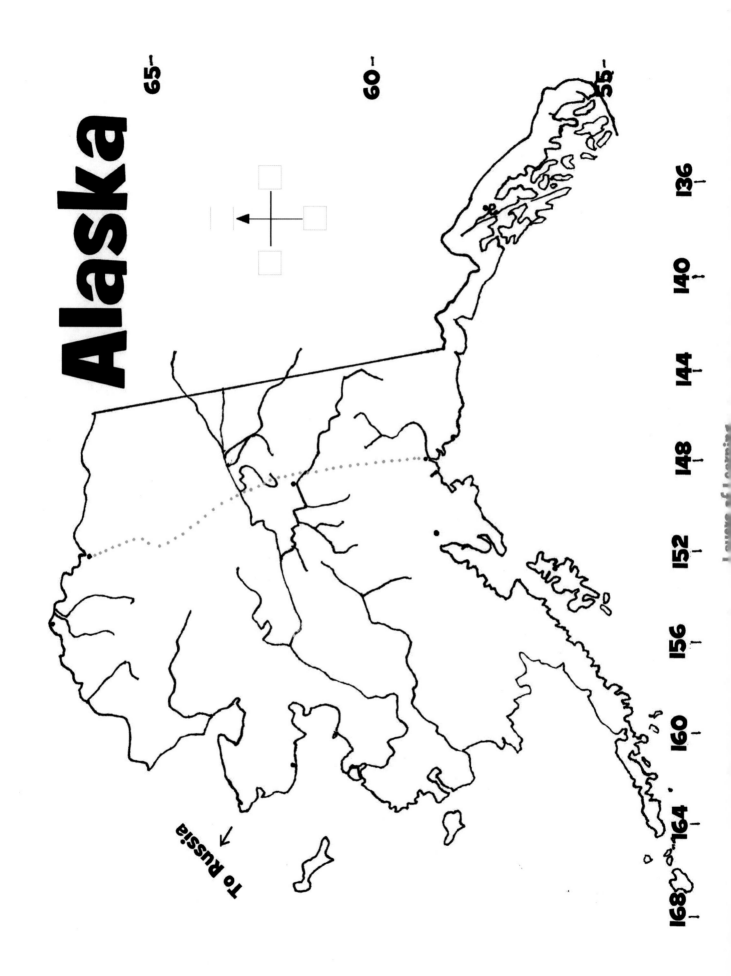

Alaska

65–

60–

55–

To Russia

168° 164° 160° 156° 152° 148° 144° 140° 136°

Alaskan Sled Dogs

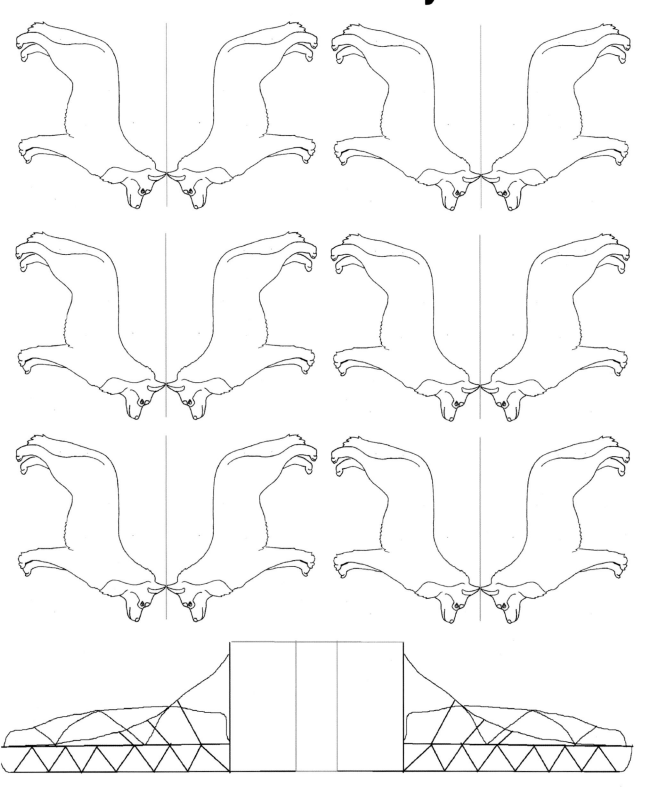

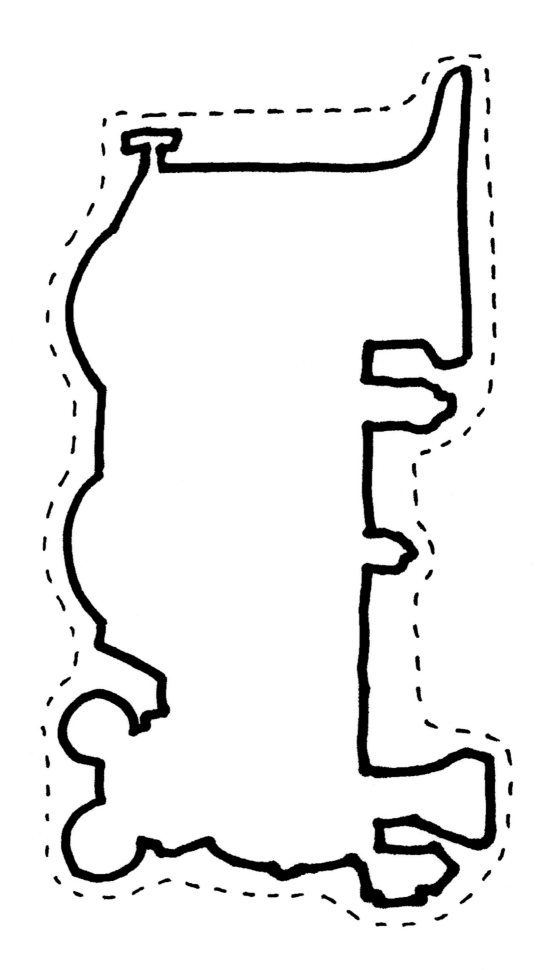

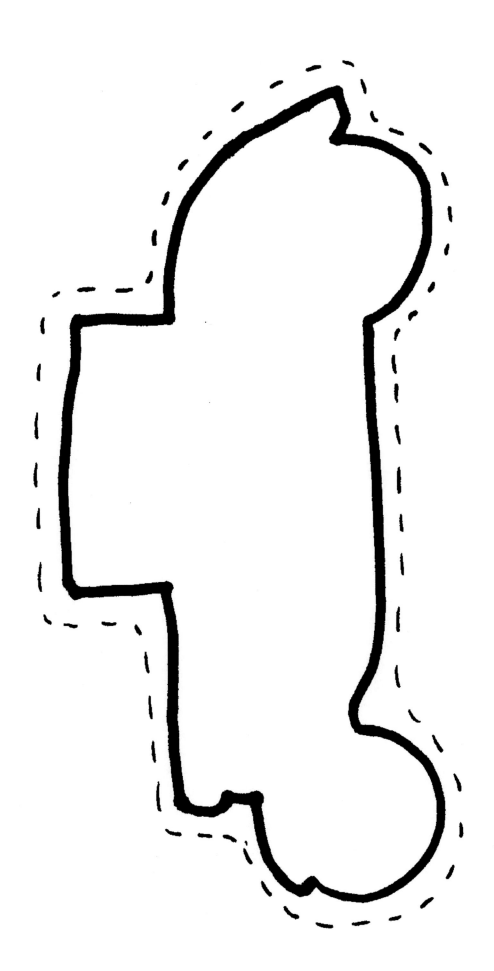

Internal Combustion Engine

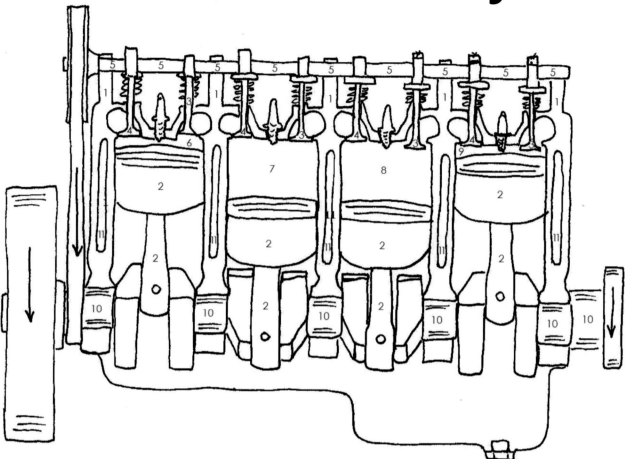

1. Black. This is the engine casing into which all the moving parts are inserted.

2. Light Blue. These are the pistons that move up and down, making the power that moves the car. The pistons are contained inside cylinders.

3. Orange. Intake valve lets both air and fuel into the cylinder where it mixes into a vapor.

4. Purple. After the fuel ignites it leaves behind exhaust, which is pushed out of the cylinder through this exhaust valve.

5. Gray. The cam shaft is a rod that turns and as it turns it pushes the valves up and down, opening and closing the air intake and the exhaust.

6. Red. A spark plug ignites the fuel, which expands rapidly, pushing the piston down.

7. Brown. The explosion ends and the piston moves back up expelling the exhaust.

8. Light Green. The piston moves back down, sucking air and fuel through the intake valve.

9. Yellow. The piston moves up, compressing air and fuel just in time for the spark to set off another explosion.

10. Green. The pistons turning causes the crankshaft to turn. The crankshaft runs to a gear box, also known as the transmission. The transmission engages causing the axle to move, which causes the wheels to move.

11. Dark Blue. The engine gets very hot with all those explosions and it must be cooled, so in most engines water is run through channels around the chambers to take away some of the heat.

What Makes A Tall Tale?

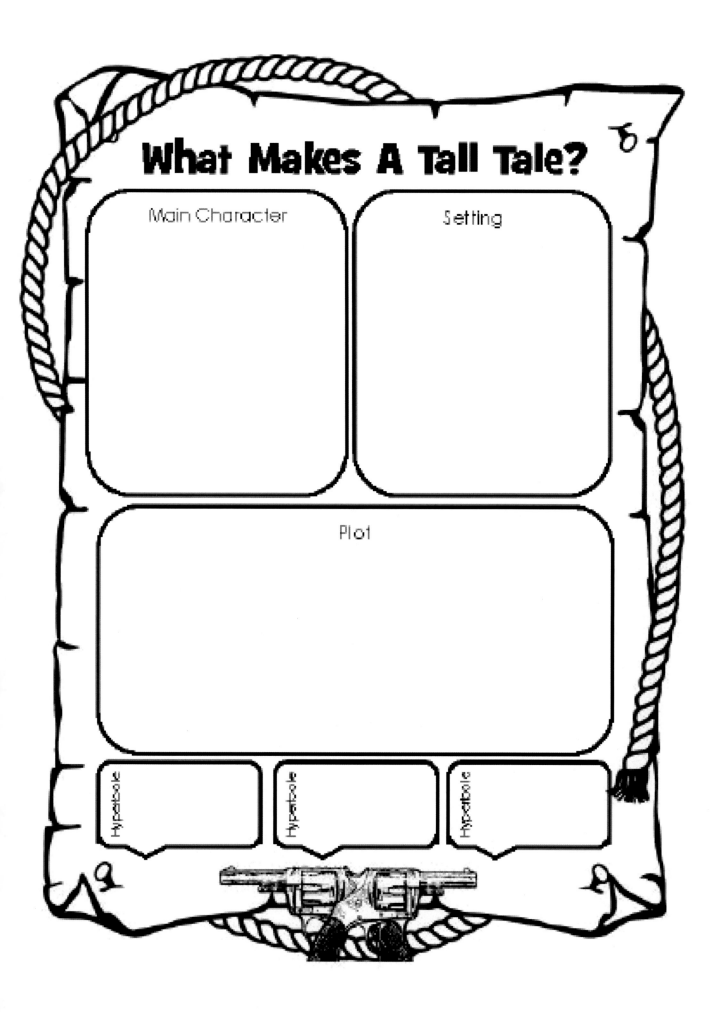

Main Character

Setting

Plot

Hyperbole

Hyperbole

Hyperbole

FLATBOAT ANNIE

Describe Flatboat Annie's appearance.

Describe Flatboat Annie's character traits.

What actions show her qualities?

What events in the tale are exaggerated?

Would you want Flatboat Annie for a friend? Why or why not?

A List of Hyperboles A Mile Long

Write and illustrate a hyperbole in each box, then check the corresponding boxes.

Does it make the story more...?
- ❑ Surprising
- ❑ Impressive
- ❑ funny

Does it make the story more...?
- ❑ Surprising
- ❑ Impressive
- ❑ funny

Does it make the story more...?
- ❑ Surprising
- ❑ Impressive
- ❑ funny

Does it make the story more...?
- ❑ Surprising
- ❑ Impressive
- ❑ funny

Does it make the story more...?
- ❑ Surprising
- ❑ Impressive
- ❑ funny

Does it make the story more...?
- ❑ Surprising
- ❑ Impressive
- ❑ funny

Does it make the story more...?
- ❑ Surprising
- ❑ Impressive
- ❑ funny

Tall Tale Template

Draw your larger than life character's head in this box, then cut out the boxes, and glue or tape them together vertically. Write your tall tale on the lines.

Tall Tale Template

Draw your larger than life character's feet in this box.

About the Authors

Karen & Michelle . . .
Mothers, sisters, teachers, women who are passionate
about educating kids.
We are dedicated to lifelong learning.

Karen, a mother of four, who has homeschooled her kids for more than eight years with her husband, Bob, has a bachelor's degree in child development with an emphasis in education. She lives in Idaho, gardens, teaches piano, and plays an excruciating number of board games with her kids. Karen is our resident arts expert and English guru {most necessary as Michelle regularly and carelessly mangles the English language and occasionally steps over the bounds of polite society}.

Michelle and her husband, Cameron, have homeschooled their six boys for more than a decade. Michelle earned a bachelors in biology, making her the resident science expert, though she is mocked by her friends for being the Botanist with the Black Thumb of Death. She also is the go-to for history and government. She believes in staying up late, hot chocolate, and a no whining policy. We both pitch in on geography, in case you were wondering, and are on a continual quest for knowledge.

Visit our constantly updated blog for tons of free ideas,
free printables, and more cool stuff for sale:
www.Layers-of-Learning.com

Made in the USA
Middletown, DE
25 May 2020